Published in Gr...
World Distribut... Limited,
P.O. Box 111, 12 Lever Street, Manchester M60 1TS,
by arrangement with Spotlight Publications Ltd.,
1 Benwell Road, London N7 7AX.

Printed in Great Britain by Jarrold & Sons Ltd., Norwich

SBN 7235 0299 4

£1·00

SPARKS NOT ABOUT TO FIZZLE OUT

SPARKS ARE more than just a flash in the proverbial pan—cisterns are being broken right left and centre whenever their name springs forth, and not only that, these oddities of popular music are beginning to steal the limelight (not to mention fans) from other great celebrities. It's true to say that they're the freshest thing since Casanova and his merry band of men, and it's undeniable that their music is so unique it cannot be compared with anyone elses. Thus they're in a class all their own. Right? Wrong, they're more than that—nobody, but nobody, can say that Sparks are just a hype and that it's just luck and a little dash of rouge and a handful of hair pins that has made them what they are today.

Just listen to their sparkling, fresh melodies and the high, hyaline vocals (courtesy of ritzy Russ Mael) and you'll see what we mean. Their overall sound is pure magic. Ron Mael's writing is amusing as well as interesting and the rest of the band are all capable of playing fine crisp and concise music on their respective instruments.

Ron says about his songwriting. "I'm inspired by lots of things. It can be the simplest theme in the world, so long as it gets to me. I like my songs to be short and sweet, why say something in twenty minutes, when it can be summed up in three?"

Their albums have all been successful, their stage acts more so.

"It can be frightening playing to pent-up teenagers whose sole aim is to grab you", exclaims Russ, the one who has to face the danger out in front. "During our last British tour I got whacked about a bit by fans, it was mind-blowing. But they don't mean to hurt you of course, it's just that they're so intent on getting you off stage they don't think they're doing you any damage."

If you haven't been to a Sparks concert, then you haven't lived (or been near to death!). The fans go balmy. They don't believe in being kitch an' all that hip stuff—If they wanna cry they cry and if they wanna wet their knicks, they wet their knicks! "I've always liked audience reaction, it helps us entertainers", opines Russ. "Like we know whether or not the audience are really digging us. If they are sombre

and solemn throughout a concert then it's nigh on impossible to tell what they're thinking!"

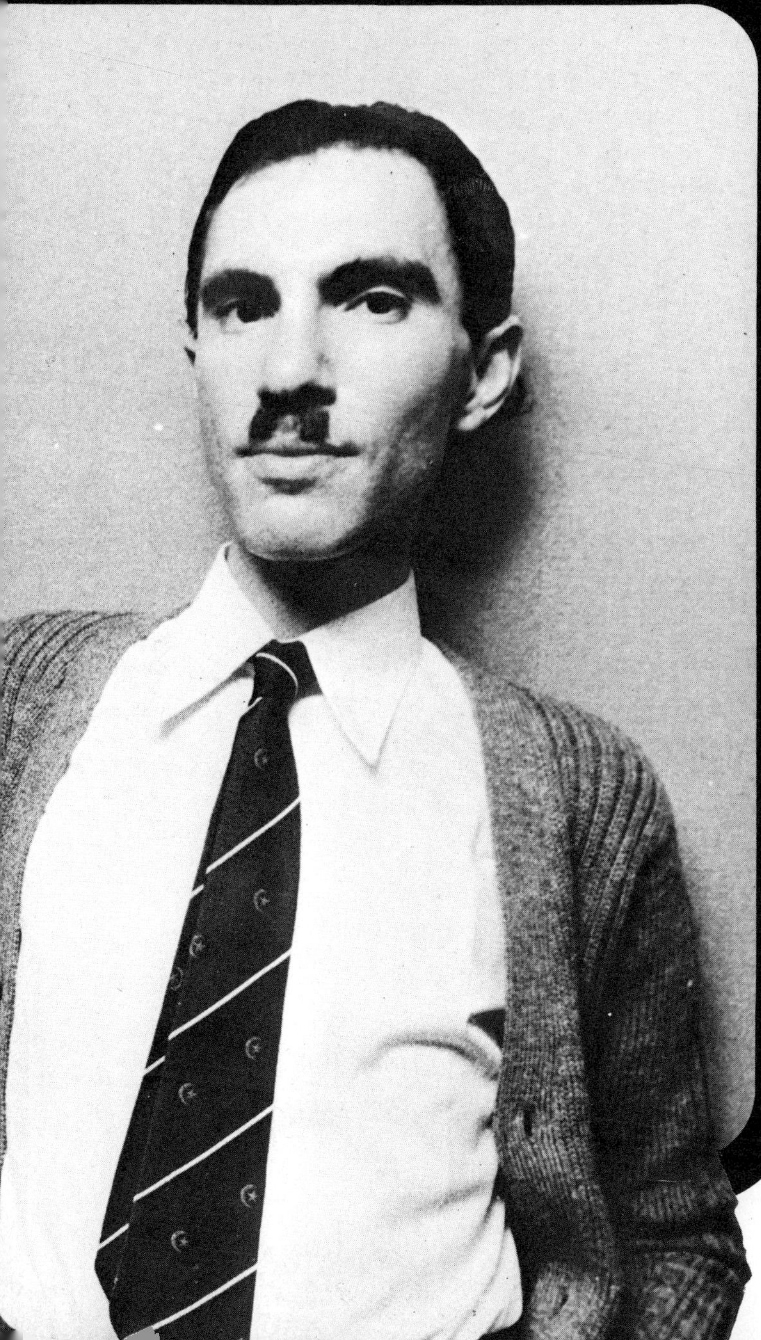

Well at least Sparks have no problems there. The kids would tear the clothes off their idols if they could, and if they did catch a glimpse of Russ's lily white flesh Gawd knows what might happen?

"We have come very near to being raped", Russ laughs casually, "but they never seem to be able to pull it off successfully."

Sparks supporters average about 15 to 16 years of age, but there has been older folk in their audiences, enjoying the band's antics (especially cherub looking Russ) just as much as their younger counterparts. Often young and old alike can be seen miming to Sparks more popular toons such as "Amateur Hour", "Girl From Germany" and "Never Turn Your Back". It's almost like a disease—the teen mania we mean. It has now spread further afield to their native America, and today they have as big a following there as they do in the British Isles.

When these two paragons of pop aren't sitting in 5 star hotel rooms waiting for their next gig, or busy over some dazzling ditty, they can be found at home, aprons on, utensils out. Ron and Russ are mad about cookin', folks (no, not actually cooking people, sweet delights more like).

Says Russ, "My speciality is sweet-after-meal-treats. When we have parties, Ron and myself usually make all these weird and delightful dishes for our guests. I'm sure most of them only come to sample the food!"

Ron also loves to collect colourful bawdy posters—and we're told he has quite a selection!

"Usually it saves writing long letters to people saying how much you miss them, when you don't. You just send them an interesting, colourful postcard and that says it all for you."

Characteristically, the two Maels are worlds apart. Russ summed it up adequately when he once said: "He's the drip", to which brother Ron replied, "Yeah, and he's the bouncy, vibrant dancey type."

If anyone cares to look into their crystal balls they'll clearly see that Sparks in general and the Mael brothers in particular are heading for super stardom—whether they planned it that way or not!

What's in a Name

HE DIDN'T stand a chance. There was already someone with the unlikely name of Gary Glitter making it, so anyone with a handle like Alvin Stardust must be jumping on the bandwagon. No chance.

But oh no, the Glitter and Stardust names were about the only similarity. There were no sequins on Alvin. On the contrary he came on dressed completely in black, and had to be a hit.

The thing about Alvin is that he has managed to sustain his success to an amazing degree. What was expected to be just a gimmicky one-off hit—My Coo Ca Choo—was really the beginning of a string of world-wide successes.

And with those successes Alvin has managed to adapt and change without losing one of his fans. Gone are the days of the black gear, though he does bring it out on special occasions.

Relaxed

Now it is a more relaxed Alvin Stardust that hits the airwaves and the concert halls. Relaxed because after years and years in the business he has finally reached the top. But he never relaxes too much, he never loses his grip on exactly what is happening in his career.

That's because Alvin remembers the old times when he wasn't Alvin Stardust, when he wasn't even Shane Fenton, but when he was Bernard Jewry.

He was more or less brought up in the show business atmosphere because when he was two his family moved from London to Mansfield where his mother opened a boarding house and used to take in the acts appearing at the local Mansfield Palace Theatre.

At the age of four he'd made his stage debut in a pantomime and from then on the "boards" were to be his life.

Two bites

He is one of the few people in pop that has had the proverbial two bites of the cherry.

The first bite came in the early Sixties when he started going on the road with the local band Johnny Theakston and The Tremeloes. He'd help hump the equipment around and occasionally sing the odd number.

The band got to the notice of the BBC and they were asked to audition for a spot on Brian Matthews' Saturday Club, and they changed the name of the band to Shane Fenton and the Fentones.

Everything seemed set and then the worst thing happened. Something that was to give our Alvin the biggest break in his career, but also something so tragic that it would stay with him for the rest of his life.

The lead singer of the band fell ill and was rushed to hospital. Two days later he died. It was a catastrophe. What on earth would they do. There was only one thing to do—call the whole thing off.

But Johnny Theakston's mother would hear none of it and she approached Alvin (then Bernard Jewry) and said that he should take over as lead singer with the band as that's what her son would have wished.

The rest becomes pop history. They passed the audition and were eventually signed up by EMI. Suddenly after the release of I'm A Moody Guy and Five Feet Two, Eyes Of Blue, they found they were stars and started touring and gigging with some of the big names in the business like Marty Wilde and Joe Brown.

Success had come tragically to Alvin but success it most certainly was and in those days he was a star.

Just when he was riding the crest of the wave he decided, like many very successful people, to give it all up. After all, he thought, performing was not for him and he went into the management side of the business.

Restless

He was a success again but still restless and eventually he had to give that up and he thought maybe he had better get out of the business altogether. But he had forgotten about the four year-old boy in the pantomime, and how the business was practically in his blood.

Run away he did, but escape—never.

He was soon back from a holiday and rarin' to get back on the boards. This time he was to be performing again.

He re-formed the Fentones and tried the cabaret circuit. Then he met Peter Shelley and was given his second bite of the cherry.

He signed with Magnet records and changed his name to the slightly ridiculous Alvin Stardust.

But there's nothing ridiculous about the success that he's achieved, and yet through it all he's remained the same old Bernard Jewry.

He knows that whatever happens he can always change his name again and get another bite of that cherry.

IN JANUARY this year Rod Stewart reached the age of thirty. To him it was an event of little significance, although he had said beforehand that he quite relished the prospect of being a man in his thirties. To the public at large, however, whenever the lead singer of a long-popular group attains that age, it in some way establishes the whole group as a musical institution.

Along with The Rolling Stones, The Hollies and Elton John, The Faces, certainly, do number among British rock's institutions and, while they don't have the same longevity as The Stones, their continued existence, defying all early predictions, is something to be proud of in itself.

From the outset, they were an unlikely combination of musical talents. Rod Stewart and Ronnie Wood came from the progressive, almost underground Jeff Beck Group, while Kenney Jones, Ian MacLagan and Ronnie Lane comprised the remnants of a straightforward commercial pop group-- The Small Faces, who had recently lost their lead singer, Steve Marriott, he having gone off to form Humble Pie.

The early days were far from easy. In Britain, the group were not generally considered a viable unit and, while in The States they were looked on with interest, "the only people who really believed in us were us," says Rod. That statement is only partially true.

Several times, Rod later admitted, he and Ron Wood were almost on the point of calling Jeff Beck and asking to go back.

Then there was the problem of Rod's solo career, on which he had already embarked when he joined The Faces. People were quick to accuse him of only using the group to further his own ends and it was widely predicted that once his own solo career was well-established, he would leave the rest of the band in the lurch and go his own way.

Now, as everyone knows, that never happened and The Faces have come to be looked on as one of the most stable bands in existence. The departure of Ronnie Lane, much later on, could have rocked the boat, but was not allowed to do so, even though when Tetsu took his place, there was for a long time much concern over whether he would be able to work with the group in Britain because of work permit and Musicians Union problems.

In the '60s, rock groups tended to be isolated units, who kept themselves very much to themselves. If a player wanted to do things outside the group to which he belonged, he was generally forced into the position of either having to swallow his private ambitions or risk all and leave. The early part of the 70s have shown an increasing amount of interplay between groups and The Faces have helped spearhead this new approach.

In his solo work Rod Stewart has been aided by people like Paul McCartney and Elton John, while Ron Wood has found time to work outside the group with the support of Keith Richard and others. Kenney Jones too has had his solo efforts.

It is remarkable that, with members of the group getting involved in so many outside musical activities, the band as a whole has never looked stronger. The disadvantages of being a group made up of musical heavies and outright commercial leftovers have, over the years, been turned into advantages. All the members of the group are now universally respected for their musicality and, without treading an awkward tightrope, the band have managed to keep both the respect of the heaviest musical critics, DJs and fans, as well as the love of much younger record-buyers.

Perhaps The Faces have the most varied audiences of any band, comprising everybody from balding longhairs to the youngest of boppers and the football crowd, the latter group finding a close affinity with Rod, who nearly had a career in professional football instead of as a musician.

In the early days the group were all looked on as ravers. They acquired a reputation for burning the candle at both ends and for having alarming capacities for alcohol. As they've grown older, however, they have become more careful. Their tour schedules are care-

facing the future

fully arranged to give them a night or two off after every three dates or so and Rod has taken particular care to avoid the voice problems that have affected so many singers.

"The muscles in the throat," he says, "are just like those in the legs. If you overstrain them, they get tense and sore and won't work properly. Spirits don't help the voice at all and so when there's a tour coming up, I go very easy on the drink.

"Also I make sure that we are never out on the road for more than three months on the trot—with rest breaks every few days. If you go on and on singing without let-up, you can do irreparable damage.

"Although the specialists have told me that I have not much reason to worry because I've got a very big larynx, I do take great care, particularly since our act contains a fair number of real belters that make a lot of demands on my voice."

Often the group opt for just the odd sprinkling of dates here and there, rather than undertake a full-scale tour all at once. Thus, it is not so surprising to learn that it was only last year that the group made their first proper tour of Europe and only their second of Britain.

As with many other top-flight groups, there is always talk of The Faces going to live abroad for tax reasons. If it does happen, it will be with much reluctance and not a little bitterness.

"The whole system is extraordinarily unfair," complains Rod. "For starters, rock has never been looked on in any way as an art to be protected and secondly governments will never take it into account that for us musicians, life can't go on forever as it is. Most of us won't still be playing when we are sixty and we are working now to provide for the rest of our lives."

Rod is only too well aware that there has to come a time to stop, but has little idea what he will do afterwards. "I dunno," he says drily, "I'm very interested in bicycles!"

1

2

3

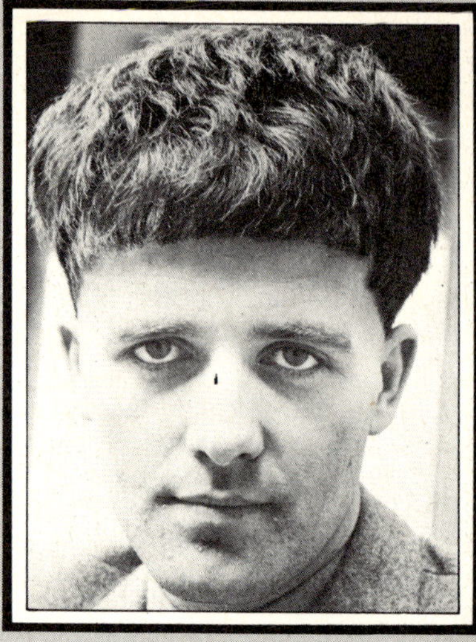

7

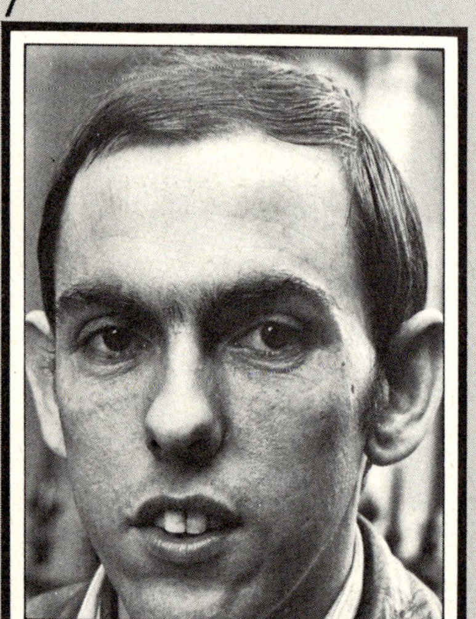

8

WITH EACH new year there comes another fashion craze; lavish hair creations and dress variations all set around the newest in make up trends.

Look back in your own photograph albums and compare your appearances of the past and your appearances of today and most probably you'll suffer from shocks, horrors or the giggles.

Can *you* spot who the following pop artists are, bearing in mind these pictures were shot many moons ago and the fashion trends then aren't what they are today.

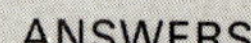

ANSWERS

Pic 1 Petula Clark

Pic 2 American pop singer, P. J. Proby in 1964.

Pic 3 Gilbert O'Sullivan in June of 1971.

Pic 4 August 1970 Olivia Newton-John; singer with 'Toomorrow' pop group.

Pic 5 Marc Bolan pictured after cutting his first disc. 17th October, 1965.

Pic 6 Anita Harris.

Pic 7 Dave Hill of Slade. Photo taken in the skinhead days.

Pic 8 Lulu.

Pic 9 D.J. Alan Freeman.

Pic 10 Ex-singing duo partnership; husband and wife, Sonny and Cher.

Pic 11 Neil Sedaka learns the trumpet.

Pic 12 The Rockin' Berries.

11

4

5

6

9

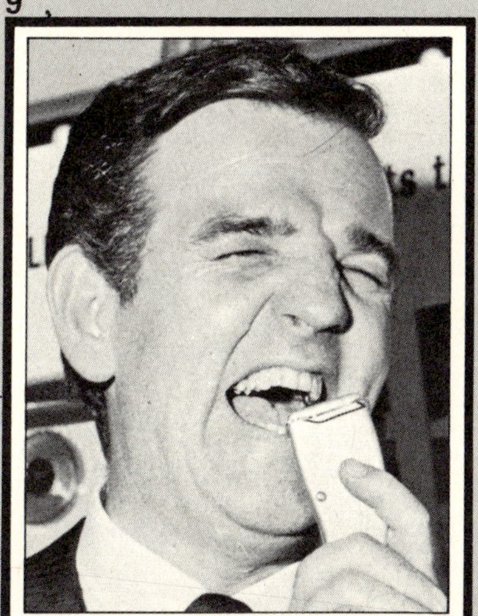

10

FACE UP TO THE PROBLEM

12

THE ACCOLADES that have been heaped on Elton John over the last couple of years range from Super Showman of the Year to Bore of the Year. Irrespective of which title you feel inclined to favour, the one thing that's inescapable is that Elton John, having reached the top, has stayed there for quite a long time. America continues to rave about him—each tour sees the previous year's record broken—and here in Britain, an Elton appearance guarantees wild crowds.

The release of his Caribou album early last year marked a peculiar water-shed in Elton's career: music critics generally felt that the album didn't make the grade. Elton's reaction was that nearly every pop star goes through stages when opinion goes against him, whether or not the criticism is warranted. Almost as if to prove the critics wrong, Elton went on later in the year to tour the States to almost fanatical acclaim, and then returned to England to find his version of the Beatles' Lucy In The Sky With Diamonds riding high in the charts, along with his Greatest Hits album.

'74 was a year of quite a few decisions for Elton—including the important one of where he was going to live. The past couple of years have seen a large number of the country's top pop/rock stars seeking sunnier and tax-freer shores, and Elton's earnings placed him at the front of the line as far as taxes were concerned. After a lot of speculation as to whether or not he was about to leap off and settle in the States, he issued a statement saying that he was going to stay in this country and pay the tax man.

When he talked about his decision later, he admitted that it hadn't really been that tough a decision to make. For all the money involved, he didn't really feel that he could live anywhere else. Having made up his mind to stay, the next problem on the agenda became looking for a new home—but around the area he's made his home for the last few years, Virginia Water.

It's a popular area for wealthy people to live in, and a lot of Elton's friends live nearby—along with one of his most important influences—his parents, who live with him. Elton's biggest problem with housing has been not having enough room—and the rumours that his garages house priceless paintings are all true.

Another reason for his wanting to buy somewhere larger is his growing passion—tennis. During his last American tour, he played a lot of tennis with people like Billie-Jean King and Jim Connors—not exactly beginners at the game—and came off quite well. Although he makes no boasts about his playing, he admits that a couple of games with people like Jim Connors teaches him far more than three weeks playing with someone of the same standard as himself. Squash is another interest, and Elton hopes to buy a house that will allow him the space to indulge in both interests.

Watford Football Club still holds

a very dear place in his heart, although his tour committments often mean he can't spend that much time with the team. When time does allow though, Elton normally goes with the team on the coach to matches, but he has doubts about his bringing luck to the team, as on the majority of occasions that he's watched the lads play, they lose!

Musically, 1975 saw the release of Elton's Captain Fantastic and the Brown Dirt Cowboy album, which was written about Elton and Bernie's experiences before they became one of the world's most successful composing duos. It was written after what amounted to nearly a year of not releasing any new material—the Greatest Hits album being a compilation of old material—and Elton felt it was one of his most important albums to date. His music during the previous year had come under some attack by the release of the Beatles' song—people asking whether Elton and Bernie had run out of material and so on. Elton's answer was that he'd often thought of releasing other people's material, but Lucy was the first time it had actually happened. He and John Lennon had worked together quite a bit in the States, both have a lot of respect for each other, and in fact John appeared on Elton's follow-up to Lucy, another Beatle hit, I Saw Her Standing There.

It was about that time that the actual name of Elton and his musicians changed to The Elton John Band, a move on Elton's part to give what he felt was due recognition to the guys who'd worked with him over the years, and the newest recruit, Ray Cooper, who's incredible talents with the tambourine and assorted percussion instruments have given a very complete sound to the band.

For Elton, one of the biggest pressures—whether for better or worse—has been his recording contract, which has meant the release of two albums a year, whether Elton and Bernie wanted to produce them or not. With his new contract, the pressure as far as it is concerned has been removed. Although during the past two or three years there have been times when Elton has resented the deadline, he now feels that perhaps the discipline was very good for him and Bernie.

It's often difficult for anyone to predict the future when applied to someone who's as successful as Elton John, but he himself feels that there are still a lot of challenges to meet. He doesn't want to pursue any other career, or even diversify his interests by tackling say, a film project, but then he's the first to admit that circumstances change constantly, and who knows what will come up. Whatever Elton does do though, it's very unlikely that he'll drop out of the public eye. Even when he's not touring or recording, photos tend to flood in of Elton jamming with assorted bands at concerts all over the country, or Elton taking over a radio show for an evening and having a bash at being a D.J. or just generally being seen about.

And with everything that he does, it's very much a case of Elton John, showman extraordinaire.

AS THE SOUND of Detroit slowly gave way to the sound of Philadelphia, so the Supremes have been replaced by the Three Degrees as the world's favourite female singing group.

And what better ambassadors of song could the Philly sound have than these three delectable ladies, whose ten year career has made them veritable pop chameleons.

They've made their music everywhere from New York's Copacabana to Caesar's Palace in Las Vegas and back to good ol' downtown Harlem.

And yet they still have time to pop over to England and check out the scene here.

Fayette Pinkney, the only original member of the group from its mid-Sixties line up is especially ecstatic about touring Britain.

"We just love it in Britain," she said on a recent visit. "I only wish we could be over here even more often than we are."

Always laughing, giggling and playing jokes on one another the Degrees seem like complete extroverts, yet Fayette hasn't always been like that.

When she was a schoolgirl in Philadelphia she kept her love for music hidden because of acute shyness. Once, in the 12th grade she even balked at performing in a High School talent show because she was too frightened to appear on the stage!

It wasn't too long after that her future manager Richard Barrett spotted her and coaxed her out from the shadows. Today Fayette is the group's specialist in melancholy ballads although she can rock and roll with the best of them.

Sheila Ferguson came into the picture in the embryonic days of the trio. Auditioned by one of her high school teachers on Barrett's behalf, Sheila originally set out to be a solo performer but blended into the Three Degrees when one of the original members opted out of showbiz.

Valerie Holiday is the only member of the trio not from Philadelphia. She joined the group after a brief singing career in her native Boston.

But now they are the perfect team dancing together on stage and singing in wonderful harmony.

They have played all the top clubs of the world to near riotous audience response and similar critical acclaim, yet they still remain three ordinary girls who just like to sing.

Their ability to blend pop and r & b has made them pop music's mistresses of pop creativity. The Three Degrees: excellent, more excellent, most excellent.

3 Degrees ~ruling supreme

LYNSEY DE PAUL ~HONESTLY

ONE THING there's never been too many of in this country—successful pop ladies. If you think about it, you can practically count them on one hand. There's Cilla, Dusty, Lulu, Olivia, Kiki Dee, Suzi—and Lynsey de Paul. And one thing that Lynsey has, as if she needed a bonus, is her talent for writing hit singles for other people as well as writing and singing them herself.

To many of the gentlemen who go out and buy singles every week, Lynsey is a number one pin-up, but when it comes to her own personal life, she keeps things pretty quiet.

Despite the fact that she is, without doubt, one of the sexiest ladies to grace the pop scene, and as such gets a lot of offers from admirers, there have only been three big loves in her life. If Lynsey does get involved, then it's totally, although she knows that however much she is involved with someone, it's important for her to have some privacy.

Being a song-writer can have extra advantages to whoever happens to be the man lucky enough to be part of Lynsey's life: songs written specially for him. Most of the songs on her widely acclaimed Taste Me Don't Waste Me album, were written about her friends—although not all of them were complimentary. There's the time that Lynsey told one admirer that she'd written a song specially for him, and then proceeded to play a track called Lying Again. Still, you can't win 'em all!

To date, Lynsey has written over a dozen hit singles, with the aid, as she's quick to point out, of her co-writer, Barry Blue. As soon as she met Barry, she established an immediate rapport, and their relationship has held firm over the years they've been working together. It's a far cry from the days when Lynsey de Paul was Lindsay Reuben and at art college and toting demo tapes round to various record companies and agencies trying to get them accepted.

Even in those days though, there was one thing that Lynsey was never without—and she still has it, and that's a dictionary of rhymes.

It might sound a slightly strange way to write songwords, but she reckons that by looking in the book she comes up with some very different rhymes that she just wouldn't think of herself. But mainly, her songs are inspired by either love or someone she knows. Even if they don't fall into either category, she believes very sincerely in what she writes, and hopes that it will give someone pleasure by listening to it.

Despite the dolly image though, Lynsey is a very shrewd business woman. Apart from her singing/songwriting, she also produces records, and it's not uncommon to find her name appearing on the credits of assorted artists' record labels. Her name is also becoming quite well-known on TV screens—including the credit for writing the theme song for the very successful John Alderton/Pauline Collins comedy show, No Honestly.

A lady with a multitude of talents is Ms de Paul, but she's also a very aware person, and someone who, despite her success, can still be easily hurt by people and experiences. It's this sensitivity that often leads her to seek what other people see as a hermit-like existence at times, but for Lynsey it's a way to get over things and to go on with the thing that matters most to her—her writing.

From Paupers to Princes

THE BAY City Rollers have every chance of going down in history and joining the ranks of the famous. Generations to come will wonder why their yester-year Earthlings found them so appealing, just as we ourselves wonder why celebrities of by-gone eras were so popular.

It must be said that these spotty faced youths have changed the whole concept of talent. It seems that their image and sex appeal are the key factors of their success. They don't write their own material (except for one or two album tracks), instead they leave it to the experts to decide which kind of boppity beat will get them into the charts. And yet with all that they're still hailed by the teeny market as the best group to emerge since the Ice Age.

Why? It's impossible for us to answer because we're not the Children of the Revolution. To the older species they represent teenage spots, out of tune voices and baggy pants. The only way to find out what lies beneath the tip of the ice-berg (metaphorically speaking), is to talk to the people who are turned on by the Rollers. And that's what we did.

Maisy, a 16 year old flaxen haired girl from Scotland says of Eric:

"He's my dream come true, my idol, my God. I thought it was just a fad, but now I've really grown to love him deeply. Other people cannot understand although I don't really expect them to. My parents think I'm crazy and the teachers at school have lectured me about my failed exams and the way my standard of work has dropped since I became a Rollers' fan. They just cannot begin to realise that Eric is the most important thing to me. They just assume that it's a puppy love and that I'll grow out of it in time. But I won't. Okay, I know I've never met Eric, but I know I shall one day. My love is so strong that I think we're fated to meet."

Well that's one fan's explanation. As you may have gathered she isn't abnormal or insensible, just a perfectly ordinary teenager in love. But there are, alas, many like her. Literally thousands of girls would give their right arm for a night with their fave Roller.

May sound frightening—even a little far-fetched, but it's perfectly true.

So what do the Rollers themselves think about this overwhelming adulation bestowed upon them? Surely it must be an awful responsibility for people so young?

Eric says. "We understand our fans perfectly well. Believe you me, we'd love to meet them all but it goes without saying that it's just impossible for us to do so. Sometimes we get very lonely stuck in our hotel rooms after a gig. We often wish that we could invite some of the fans to the hotel just for a friendly chat. But it might do more harm than good."

Tam Paton, the Rollers' personal manager puts it like this. "To those girls the Rollers are special. They're not like the boys next door. But if they were to act in an ordinary fashion then they would undoubtedly lose their appeal. It's logical. Let me explain it in this way. If you can't have something which you really crave for you want it all the more, right? Then, when you finally get it, nine times out of ten it's disappointing. Idealism is nicer than realism, but usually people cannot live up to other people's fantasies of them, no matter how fantastic they are."

So is that what makes them so

special? Being like elusive butterflies or china dolls in a shop window? (Both of which can be stared at but not touched.) Are the guys happy with this kind of situation?

Leslie pauses for a second to weigh up the matter. "Not always", he says slowly. "There are times when I become really depressed and think how nice it would be to have a steady girl to come home to, a person you know would love you even if you were a tramp in the gutter, not because you're a pop star.

"Before I joined the Rollers I used to have my fair share of birds running after me y'know just like any normal guy, but it wasn't like it is now."

Woody cuts in, "It's a bit like being a bum one minute and a millionaire the next. When you hadn't any money people just didn't want to know, and then once you're rich all these smiling, pseudo-friendly people start appearing from nowhere and want to get to know you."

Well that's how it is right now, and probably will be for some years to come. For it looks as though the Rollers have at least another demi-decade at the top. But what about when they're on the decline? Everyone who rises must fall.

"We just don't think about that," they all say. "Why look that far ahead when we're living for now? We all know that someday we shan't be at the top, but hopefully we'll have enough money to live comfortably and in a style that suits us. When the time comes it won't be all that difficult to hand the throne over to somebody else."

Queen

...regal rock

WHEN, in 1973, that awful expression 'Glam Rock' was enjoying its heyday and bisexuality was tout à la mode, a new name emerged on the scene—Queen. Groaning journalists got ready to write this group off as the grossest outfit to climb belatedly on the bandwagon of glittery decadence.

Few writers, though, would pass up the chance of an interview with the band. With a name like that, the burning question to be answered was 'Are they or aren't they?'

It rapidly transpired that they weren't and in those days were anxious to play down the gay connotation of the name.

"It's all very embarrassing," Queen's lead singer Freddie Mercury would say at the time. "Actually we've been around quite a while and we chose our name long before glam rock and the gay thing became fashionable. We like to think of ourself as Queen in the regal sense, because our music is supposed to be quite majestic in a way."

Even in those early days, Queen had plenty of interesting things to say about themselves apart from inviting speculation over their sexual proclivities.

Before the group ever formed, each of its members had 'further-educated' themselves to the hilt and armed themselves with degrees that would give them passports to very respectable careers should their venture into music ever fail.

Like the countless girls who take secretarial diplomas before launching into the precarious world of the theatre, Queen decided to have something behind them to fall back on should the worst ever come to the worst.

Like most new groups, Queen, at the outset, were far from wealthy and rather than furnish themselves with second-rate equipment which was all they could afford, they decided they'd do better to make their own. Between them they had considerable expertise with electrics and so, rather than their home-made guitars becoming an object of patronising talk, they were scrutinised with much real interest and hailed in some quarters as genuinely innovatory.

Their costumes were also quite novel, since they were probably the first group to abandon the garish multi-coloured clothes that had run rife through the pop world in favour of outfits all in black and white, leaving lights to provide the colour. This move was quickly picked up by so many other bands that very soon black and white costumes became as commonplace as what had gone before.

Queen's first album "Queen 1" was received with mixed feelings, but the general opinion was that it wasn't at all a bad start.

Onstage it was clear that, however much Queen might protest that their name was to be taken in the regal sense, the other applied equally well. There was a strong air of high camp about the whole of Freddie's stage presence, culminat-

ing in an interpretation of Shirley Bassey's *Big Spender* that would have suited a drag queen down to the ground!

In the autumn of 1973 Queen did their first major British tour supporting Mott The Hoople. Mott, who had only recently hit the big time themselves, were only too aware of the difficulties of being a second-on-the-bill band and, seeing the potential in Queen, did everything possible to make the new boys feel at home and the two bands rapidly became best of friends.

That tour helped Queen immeasurably. By the time it was over, their act had become much more polished and generally more confident all round, they'd weeded out the weak links in their material and were ready to go out as a headlining band in their own right.

They had been seen and approved by thousands of people up and down the country and had successfully paved the way for their second album "Queen 11" to go into the charts and they also had a huge hit with a somewhat unlikely single called *Seven Seas Of Rhye.*

By Christmas 1973 everyone was tipping Queen as *the* brightest hope for 1974 and so they were to prove.

By Easter last year they had arrived to stay but, even at that time, few realised how much higher they would go.

In the late summer they suffered a setback when Brian May contracted jaundice and they had to cancel an American tour. It wasn't to hold them up for long though.

Soon after his recovery they came out with a single, *Killer Queen,* that would have been worthy of The Beatles and followed it with their third album "Sheer Heart Attack", which immediately shot into the upper regions of the charts. Meanwhile, on a new British tour, they sold out everywhere they played and the audience reaction everywhere was ecstatic. In what was generally considered a lean time for roadshows with many top line bands playing to half-full houses, only two acts stood out as generating real enthusiasm on the scale of Beatle days—one was David Essex, the other Queen.

This year Queen have been since virtually everywhere that matters, from the Far East to America's West Coast and the reaction everywhere has been tremendous. In some places where they were playing for the first time, they were already well known. In Japan, for example, they'd already been voted top band with "Sheer Heart Attack" as top album, before they'd ever set foot in the place.

While the band has never had a leader as such, Freddie has come to be looked on as its main spokesman. He's developed a lovely line in camp humour and now, when any one asks him 'Are you gay?', he blithely replies 'As a daffodil my dear, as a daffodil' and delights in telling stories of embarrassed customs men who open his cases to be confronted with bottles of mascara and nail polish among piles of satin knicks.

It's all just good clean fun though. If it weren't, you wouldn't see, at Queen concerts, the legions of mums and dads who now make up a solid part of the group's devoted following. Perhaps soon they'll invent another ghastly tag for bands such as Queen . . . could it be 'Pantomime Rock' with Freddie as the good fairy?

SLADE-

IN 1975 Slade have emerged from one of the more difficult periods in their history when, for about two years, things weren't going all their way.

First there was the terrible crash in 1973 that killed the girlfriend of drummer Don Powell and nearly proved fatal for Don himself. After he'd recovered from his physical injuries he was found to be suffering from amnesia and, once back at work with the group again, there was all the trouble of having to learn songs again, that beforehand he had been playing for ages.

After Don's recovery, Slade made a triumphant return but then last year there was a bit of a lull and people began to talk of Slade as being on their way out. Perhaps the famous Noddy Holder voice was becoming just a little too familiar, perhaps the group were not quite in touch with the new developments that were springing up around them.

Slade were not to be dismissed that easily. While they fully recognised that no group can expect number one hits as their divine right forever, they reckoned they still had an important part to play both in the charts and as one of the most exciting live bands that this country has spawned.

Gradually they began to tailor their music to meet the public's new tastes and the heavy stomping singles of the past gave way to more melodic compositions like *Far Far Away* and so the hits have gone on.

Slade have always been one of the hardest-working bands in existence and have played all the major venues there are to be played, often several times. Late last year the group decided to take their music to parts of the country that very seldom are honoured with a visit from a rock group at all and they've been continuing that policy this year.

Slade have always been anxious to make sure that all their fans have the opportunity of seeing them live, which is why they've kept up such a heavy work schedule. Also they've never lost touch with their fans by becoming remote superstars, who can only be glimpsed outside concert halls dimly through the smoked glass windows of a limousine.

They like nothing more than to be treated as ordinary people by fans who feel able to identify closely with them. "I think our favourite gig ever," says Noddy, "was the Isle of Arran. We used to play there every holiday and we kept it up for two years. We'd stay there and actually walk to gigs. At opening time we'd all be in the pub and we weren't due to play until after they shut. By that time everybody was feeling very mellow so we had a great time. You look back on that sort of gig with nostalgia, because these days it isn't really possible—much as we'd like it to be.

Without being encouraged, audiencies have always participated in Slade concerts by singing along with the group on the choruses.

"It's a marvellous feeling," says Noddy, "particularly when you are in a foreign country where the fans don't speak English, and they know all the words and sing them along with you.

"It's particularly gratifying when one of their favourites happens to be one of your's and you've written the song yourself. We make a point of not necessarily playing what we want to play but what we think the fans want to hear."

Right from the early days of Slade, they've attracted hordes of

still very much a force to reckon with

football fans, which is curious because the group don't claim to be football mad themselves.

"When we tour around the country," says Don Powell, "kids come up to us and talk about football teams and we don't really know anything about it. We let them tell us. I can't really say that we are football fans ourselves, because we don't really have that much time to get stuck into it. We do watch TV at the weekends sometimes to see what's going on and we invariably watch important matches like World Cup games or the Cup Final. I think Noddy's more expert on the game than the rest of us, I prefer athletics myself."

Slade are such a busy band that they very seldom get much free time to go and see any other groups. On the rare occasion they do it's usually because the band they see is sharing the bill with them.

When they do get a bit of time off, the boys are often to be found socialising together. "We always go out together when we're not working," says Don. "We ring each other up and go to the pub back home or go for a meal or round to each other's places."

For a long time the whole group lived in their home town of Wolverhampton, but gradually and, almost reluctantly, they've acquired homes in London simply for convenience's sake.

Last year the group finally got around to making their first film "Flame", which was released early this year. The film was very carefully researched beforehand, as Don explains. "The director and scriptwriter toured with us and got to know each of us individually so that when it was written our separate identities came out true.

"When we made the film at first we were very worried that the professional actors in it might look down on us, but it was not really like acting, more just talking amongst ourselves. When we were with the actors it did seem a little strange at first and for the first couple of days we found ourselves fluffing lines and missing cues because of it."

The film was generally well-received and of course was a must for all true Slade fans, but perhaps the timing of its release was a little unfortunate, since it came out at around the same time as Ken Russell's "Tommy", which, in a way, tended to overshadow "Flame". Nevertheless, that couldn't really be helped and Slade are keen to continue making films as and when the right script comes along and they can make time to do it in between their hefty touring and recording commitments.

In the meantime, you'll notice, nobody this year has made the mistake they did last year of writing Slade off as a spent force.

On the Road

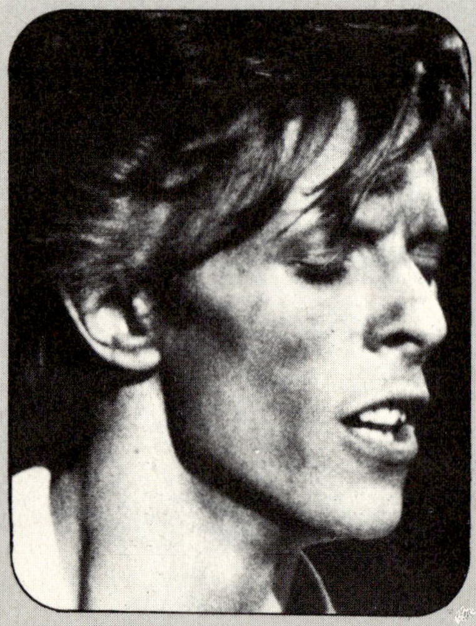

IN AMERICA, where just about every kind of music gets radio play, live performances are perhaps not essential to selling records, although everybody goes out and plays somewhere at sometime. Here, however, with much more restricted airplay, concerts are a must for anybody who wants to get anywhere.

Among the established greats, only one person springs to mind who has never set foot on a British stage—Elvis Presley and even he probably wishes that he had not put off coming for so long that any concert of his here would now be an anti-climax.

Some artists adore touring, others loathe it, but either way there's no doubt that there's very little glamour about it and that it's damned hard work.

For a star rock performer to perform before their fans is quite a different business from a star actor or actress doing the same thing. The actor generally works in one West End theatre for as long as their play may run with a dressing room befitting their status at their disposal. Rock stars, on the other hand, go out to their audiences all over the country, playing in halls that are often ill-equipped for the purpose and using dressing rooms that are anything but luxurious.

Then there is the travelling, involving not only the stars themselves but all their equipment, baggage and touring staff.

Of course, the process of getting round the country varies from group to group. A modest acoustic outfit may have little difficulty with their equipment, while getting ELP's tons of gear from one gig to another is worse than moving house every day.

New groups are often not in a position to call the tune over the facilities they require and lack the experience to know how to do so anyway with the result that they frequently find themselves getting a raw deal all round. Often you will read of them complaining after a disastrous gig that they never even had the opportunity to do a sound check beforehand.

More experienced bands have learned to make sure that their requirements are met and that the whole touring business goes reasonably painlessly. Some, like The Rolling Stones, have made an art out of getting their show on the road.

Mick Jagger, who is a brilliant organiser, draws up lists of exactly what his band will require all the way along the line and these days somebody is employed for months before a tour simply to make sure that all Jagger's wishes are met.

The Stones' stipulations go far beyond the kind of things that most bands expect like hot and cold running water in dressing rooms with proper amounts of soap and towels.

If a promoter wants The Stones, he must undertake to provide at each venue a vast quantity and variety of alcohol plus a veritable feast of food, with all necessary cutlery and crockery. The group have suffered in the past from touring on an unvaried diet of take-away chicken legs and booze out of a beaker and are in a position to demand better.

In the past rock groups became notorious for smashing up hotels and dressing rooms. Sometimes that kind of behaviour can be attributed to sheer frustration over inadequacy of service, sometimes

to ill-contained high spirits after a successful concert.

Most rock stars these days use limousines to transport themselves and their musicians from one gig to another, though every now and again a major name gets slated for travelling in the luxury of a limousine, while leaving his backing musicians to travel together in a van. Over longer distances, most stars use planes for quickness, though David Bowie, for one, has a dread of flying and invariably crosses the sea by boat and land by car, bus or train. Hence, he can be weeks getting from one side of the world to the other, as was the case when after a tour of the Far East, he headed back westwards via the spartan Trans-Siberian Railroad.

In general, a typical tour day goes something like this. At the crack of dawn the road crew will remove the band's gear from where they played the previous evening (if they haven't already done so the night before) and drive to the next town.

The band themselves will follow on later and check into their new hotel before inspecting the venue and having a sound check late in the afternoon.

Sound checks are normally conducted behind locked doors with just the band and their sound crew present. Journalists are seldom admitted, partly because sound checks are often tempestuous, and partly because bands frequently use them to try out new numbers in secret.

Once the sound check is complete, the band will return to their hotel for something to eat before going to the hall again for the gig. In the case of a really big name group, there often has to be a conference about security with perhaps a quick, safe getaway being planned for after the concert is over.

Once the gig is over, the band will return once again to their hotel for more food. After that things vary. A few artists are confirmed early-to-bed people, others seldom fail to have a party of some sort, or sit up half the night drinking and talking or giving interviews. Often stars who are scarcely ever "available" for interviews in London can successfully be cajoled into talking in hotels in some far-flung region of the country.

The next day the same process happens all over again. Some dread the whole business, others treat it all as one long party or cart their families around with them to preserve some semblance of normality. But whatever any of them think of it, they all have to undergo it sometime.

JUST FOURTEEN short years ago Steveland Morris was brought to Motown by Ronnie White of the Miracles. His name was changed to Stevie Wonder and he was billed as a genius.

No one could take the tag seriously. O.K. he was blind, he played good harp, but a genius . . .

Now he's proving just how far ahead he is of most other performers in the soul, jazz or rock fields, and that genius tag looks as if it really was true all along.

Being blind, Stevie is more aware of things that go on around him and this is translated into his music, and he often does things that only people who can see need do.

For instance he turns the lights on an off when he goes to the bathroom. What for? you might ask. He says it's 'cos he hears everybody else do it. Click, you go in. Click, you're out. So he does it too.

There are many stories of Stevie's awareness.

His assistant Ira Tucker relates: "I remember one time we were in Puerto Rico and it was a sunshiney day.

"Stevie said it was going to rain. He said he could smell the moisture in the air and we were all laughing at him. Three hours later, sure enough, it came. A hailstorm!"

Born in Saginaw, Michigan, Stevie's family moved to Detroit in his early years. He never let the fact that he was blind separate him from other kids.

"In fact I got in more trouble than most sighted kids, sneaking girlfriends to the railroad tracks . . . always running around," he recalls.

"I never knew what it was to see, so it's just like seeing. The sensation of seeing is not one that I have and not one that I worry about."

The story of his rise to fame from his first No. 1 hit single Fingertips to the present day is well known. But it is surprising that it was when he was 21 and legally received all his childhood earnings that his music also matured and he began to use different concepts and go in different directions.

But Stevie denies he was trying to be different. "I'm just trying to be myself," he said at the time.

He's always seeking new challenges. He wishes he could drive a car and says he will one day.

"I've flown a plane before," he adds. A Cessna or something from Chicago to New York. Scared the hell out of everybody.

"The pilot was there and he just let me handle this one thing and I say 'what's' this' and we went whish, whoop."

Oh yes, Stevie likes challenges all right.

He adds: "Being blind, you don't judge books by their covers; you go through things that are relatively insignificant and you pick out things that are more important.

"People shouldn't expect a set thing from me—I love to grow."

So we've noticed: you've gone from Little Stevie Wonder to one of the biggest stars around.

STEVIE ....WONDER STAR

LEO SAYER

–HE DO LIKE TO BE BESIDE THE SEASIDE

BRIGHTON'S SEDATE and upper class neighbour, Hove, houses many distinguished residents, among them knights and dames of the theatre, distinguished writers and artists. There also lives one of rock's newer superstars, Leo Sayer.

Leo was brought up in Brighton's posh suburb, married there and has made his home there. "My wife loves the place," he says, "and I like remaining there among all the friends I grew up with. Life in London holds no attraction for me."

While he's writing, Leo spends most of his time at his seaside home, nipping into London only when needs must for interviews or travelling the country for gigs when he has to do so.

But, living with the wife he loves, in the town he loves best, Leo is not an entirely happy person. "I'm a pretty miserable sort of character," he confesses and points out how his pessimism has inspired many of his songs. "My main fear is that one day the time might come when I'm so happy, rich and famous that there won't be anything left to write about."

Leo's career began the day he met Dave Courtney. Dave was auditioning bands for an agency he hoped to open in Brighton and was beginning to despair of finding any new talent when he heard Leo. He was immediately taken by Leo's unusual voice and phrasing and signed him on the spot. Soon the agent/artist relationship was dispensed with and the pair of them started working as songwriters.

Dave took their tapes to Adam Faith, the man who had had an extremely successful pop career before turning to acting and finding new fame as "Budgie" on TV. Adam offered to manage Leo's career and began looking for a convenient studio to begin recording work.

The nearest was Roger Daltrey's private studio a few miles along the Sussex coast. There they began work and when Roger heard the first results, he was so impressed that he commissioned the two unknown songwriters to pen all the material for his solo album.

Leo was amazed. "I'd always thought my songs would be far more suitable for a middle of the road singer like Andy Williams than for a rock singer from a band like the Who." The results, though, were phenomenal and provided Daltrey both with a hit album and single *Giving It All Away*.

The reflected glory was more than enough to launch Leo's career, not just as a songwriter, but recording artist and live performer as well. He quickly had a hit with his first album "Silverbird" and a string of single successes.

At first he took the unusual step, onstage, of hiding his face behind pierrot make-up to emphasise the pathos in his songs. To continue doing so for long though would have restricted him to a single visual presentation and anyway it was impracticable since it took a full hour to apply.

So, dispensing with stage make-up, he settled for a costume reminiscent of the days of Jolson.

Today Leo Sayer is an international star with a string of worldwide hits behind him and more and more attention being paid to his work, particularly in America.

He says that now he'd like to concentrate less on song-writing and more on the performing side of his career, but you can be sure that he won't be away on tour for too long at a time. The call of his beloved Sussex seaside is too strong.

THE BEATLES ...then and now

EARLIER THIS year the most famous group of all time finally broke up.

Though they hadn't recorded together for more than four years they had still been tied by financial considerations.

It took the Beatles a long time to die, but no one shed that many tears because out of the band came four startlingly individual musicians who still manage to make some of the finest music in the world.

John Lennon was always acknowledged as the leader of the Beatles and something of a unique personality who commits himself totally to whatever cause he believes in—whether it be peace or revolution.

He has taken to living in New York, a city admirably suited to his temperament, where he is free to express himself 24 hours a day in the world's most intense metropolis.

Always willing to put himself on the line John has come in for more criticism from the music press than any of the others. Some call his music honest, some pretentious.

But whichever way you look at it, a new release by John Lennon is still something of an event as he blends hard, gritty rock songs with laid-back wistful melodies.

Imagine really did catch both the imagination and the sales though his follow-up *Sometime In New*

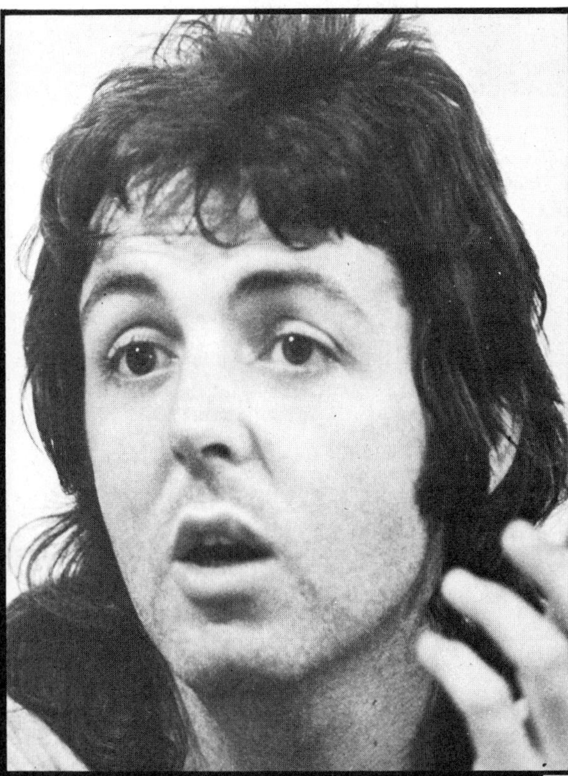

York City got panned by many critics.

Walls And Bridges saw him back at the top again. Now he is more popular in the States than he is in Britain where he really is the peaceful revolutionary.

George Harrison has more things in common with John than might at first be envisaged. Apart from the fact that they both believe in peaceful means to achieve an end, both John's marriage to Yoko Ono and George's to Patti Boyd recently broke up with a consequent blaze of publicity.

But for all Beatle fans, George will always be the mystic.

When the band went to India in the Sixties to find out more about eastern religions and meditation, it had a deep and lasting effect on lead guitarist George.

He immediately sensed the different consciousness needed to understand the new concepts being taught him by the Indian gurus.

And these were to be given a prominent place in his subsequent music. He learnt to play sitar adequately and became great friends with Ravi Shankar, whom he was later to tour with.

George was the recluse of the band though since his recent tour and album he's started having more of a social life.

He's the original "seeker" and his songs are full of praise for Rama and Shiva. He lives in the shadow of his God.

Some of his tunes are as good as anything John or Paul have ever written and are destined to become standards.

But if George was the religious Beatle then surely Ringo was the lovable clown.

Musically speaking he is the weakest of the four. His drumming was never in the Ginger Baker class, and one of the good things about Ringo is that he would be the first to admit it.

He makes the less serious albums of the four, but that's not to devalue the music on them. He's shrewd enough never to try to outstep his talent and that's one of the reasons he's still up there in the singles charts with everything he releases.

If it's good, happy, danceable music you want, Ringo can provide it with the help of some of the most famous musicians around.

When he's not in the recording studio he's over the road in the film studio and it's probably in this line that he will eventually settle.

His role in That'll Be The Day was remarkable indeed and caused quite a few eyebrows to raise in the States where critics are quick to say that he's a no talent. Ringo proved them wrong and looks like continuing to dumbfound them for some time to come.

Now then, Paul McCartney. Well, Wings have become the most prestigious and famous offshoot of the old Beatles, yet when Paul first went solo he was also attacked mercilessly.

For a start he was blamed for the break-up of the old band and that seemed too much to take at the time.

Only now are his early solo albums like Ram being rediscovered for the gems that they are.

It was Band On The Run that was to change everything for Paul McCartney. In one fell swoop he came up with the best album that any of the former Beatles had produced since they went solo.

Something to rank with Abbey Road and Sgt. Pepper. It was to spur John Lennon on to make his best solo album.

Unlike the other Beatles, Paul's marriage continues to work and Linda is now an integral part of the Wings set-up. He has written a wide variety of songs from rockers to film music, but everything has that indefinable McCartney quality.

He is quite simply one of the best and most innovative musicians this country has produced.

But then all four of them come into that category or they wouldn't have been—the Beatles.

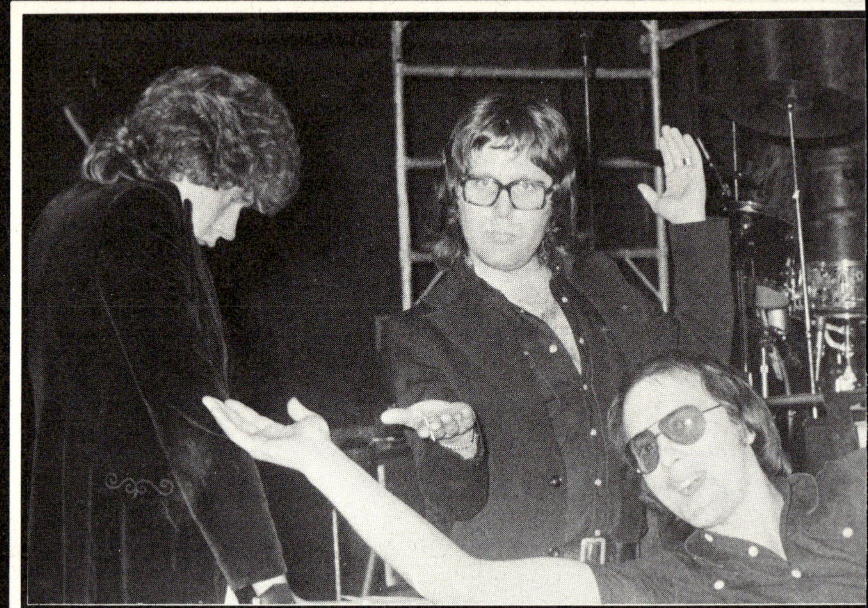

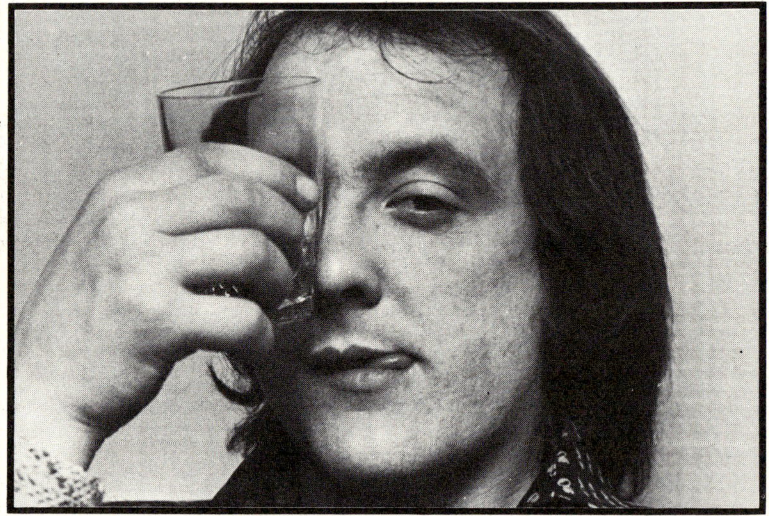

WHEN MUD first began having number one hit singles, they surprised not only the whole music business, which is well used to being proved wrong, but also the team who write their hits for them—Messrs Nicky Chinn and Mike Chapman.

When Nicky and Mike began writing for Mud, they'd already been providing Sweet with hits for a long while and couldn't see Sweet being anything but their top-selling artists. "Sweet," pronounced Mike Chapman, "will be the group to provide us with the number one hits. Mud will have plenty of top ten successes, but they aren't really in quite the same league."

Very soon Mike had to eat his words. Mud began racing Sweet to the top of the charts—and getting there first. They also quickly acquired something that had always eluded Sweet—the respect of the "heavier" rock critics. Sweet, to be fair, had always had the most appalling bad luck when critics turned out in force for one of their gigs. Somehow on those nights something always managed to go wrong with the sound system so that they were never heard to best advantage with the result that time and time again their concerts were roundly slated.

Mud were much luckier. At important gigs things went smoothly from the start and even the most sceptical critics could not deny

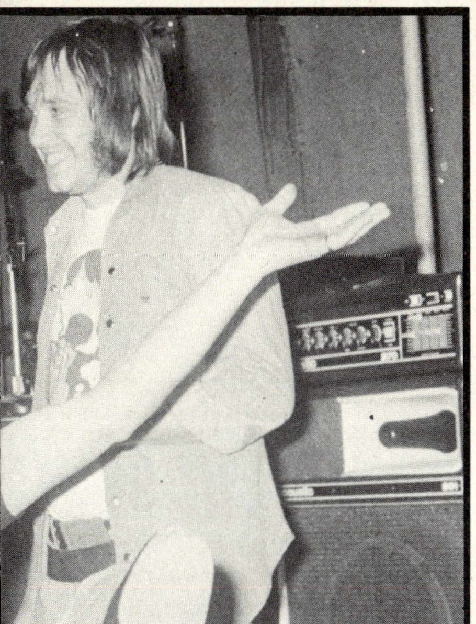

CAUTION ~there's Mud around

that Mud could play as well as the best of them. This resulted in them being featured heavily in papers that normally wouldn't touch so blatantly a commercial band.

All the members of the group came from in or around Mitcham in Surrey and they'd all known each other, at least vaguely, since childhood. The name of the group was chosen for them by their lead guitarist, Rob Davis. "At the time," he explains, "we were all wearing kind of mud-coloured suede jackets, which gave me the idea. It proved to be a good name, because we always got big billing on posters advertising concerts even when we were way down the list. Among groups with longer names, our's really stood out because, with only three letters, they had to print it bigger."

So Mud stuck (sorry) in people's minds, but they still had a long way to go before their first hit. Their first recording deal failed to provide any chart success for them at all, so after a while they bought themselves out of it for only a couple of hundred pounds or so. It was a good thing the escape didn't cost them more, because they simply didn't have it. While just managing to earn a living wage, they were scarcely living in the lap of luxury. Often Rob Davis's dad would drive the boys to gigs in his beaten up old Wolseley just to help out.

"Fortunately," says Rob, "we were all living at home with our own families, who were most understanding so we never had to go hungry."

After they bought themselves out of their first contract, Mud went to see Mickie Most, who'd produced hits for countless artists and ran his own highly successful RAK label.

Mickie found them some songs, but they weren't right for the group and Mickie agreed that they weren't, so none of them were ever recorded.

Eventually Mickie introduced Mud to Chinn and Chapman, who readily agreed to take them under their wing. Then came their first hit *Crazy* and all the huge successes that have followed. Very soon they joined the small band of primarily singles groups who manage also to sell albums in large quantities.

They were one of the first groups to make the most of television's main showcase for pop artists "Top Of The Pops", working out special routines for each successive single to bring out the fun element in their music. Visual presentation and all round entertainment has always figured in their minds just as much as the music itself.

There comes a time in the life of every straight commercial pop group when its members long to spread their wings and try something adventurous away from what has come to be expected of them. Mud could well be pardoned for a little self-indulgence at this stage in their careers and there's no doubt that they have the musical skill to accomplish something quite ambitious, but they prefer to keep their feet firmly on the ground and take things very gently.

"Of course we would like to progress a little," they say, "but as long as we are making good singles and albums we are content. We always have to keep in mind that our fans expect entertainment from us as well as just music and we don't think they'd like to think of us taking ourselves too seriously."

They have begun, however, to expand the field of their activities a little. This year saw their film debut in "You're Never Too Young To Rock" with, among others, Peter Noone, The Glitter Band and The Rubettes. It's a perfect first film vehicle for them, since it gives them a chance to present their talents without having to change their image drastically.

While fully appreciative of the help that their team of songwriters have given them in the past, Mud are now using other writers and songs. All the members of the band have been writing separately and together for some time and are gradually infiltrating more of their own numbers into their act.

Privately, they all live modest existences. Until recently, most of them still lived with their families and when they finally did leave the nest it was not for the huge houses in the country, in which some stars invest, but conveniently situated flats of unpretentious proportions. Caution in everything seems to be the watchword.

"WHAT IS soul?" asked Ben E. King in one of his bigger hit records of the late Sixties. What indeed!

Any pop fan today would be able to answer that one. It's the black music that has started creeping up the charts in recent years, marking a significant turnaround in musical taste.

Once it was a very specialised field of music with its devout followers knowing everything even down to the matrix and logo numbers of individual discs.

But suddenly black is not only beautiful it's also big business with stars like Aretha Franklin, Gladys Knight and James Brown amongst the highest paid in the world.

One of the reasons why soul music has broken so big is the existence of discotheques where black music is almost exclusively played—the irresistable beat, the raw emotional feeling of the records, and the honesty of the music means you just have to dance along.

SOUL SPECTRUM

Soul has had its boom periods before—particularly in the middle Sixties with the emergence of Tamla Motown completely dominating the scene.

Strangely enough, it was those "soulful" gentlemen, the Beatles, who did a lot to publicise black music and get it accepted by the British public.

Before anyone had ever heard of Berry Gordy or Smokey Robinson, Messrs. Lennon and McCartney were talking ecstatically about people like the Marvelettes and Mary Wells and this whole thing that was happening in the States with black artists becoming more revered.

They even went on to record Please Mr. Postman—a Marvelettes hit song in America.

But no matter how much publicity you give a thing, it won't be accepted unless it can stand up on its own merits.

It was to take another 10 years before soul music would be in that position.

Now not only has Motown music—the original sound of Detroit's ghettoes—been completely accepted by the buying public, it has almost become passé—establishment. The days when Detroit and Memphis, with its Stax sound, were the only two credible areas of soul music is long gone.

In its place there is Philadelphia, courtesy of maestro producers Gamble and Huff, the Florida sound of young Howard Casey, and the even more involved West Coast sound of people like Sly Stone and Larry Graham of Graham Central Station.

Yet how did it all begin? In many ways soul is much nearer the natural feeling of today, than rock or folk for instance.

It was born out of that common stock of musical influences—the Blues, and evolved as the black man in America became more and more urbanised, and the rural feeling of the blues gave way to the more polished and sophisticated expression of soul music.

Indeed, rock music also stemmed from the blues with white men in the middle Fifties beginning to play black "race" music and calling it rock 'n roll. Blacks had been listening to the same thing for years.

Nowadays soul music and rock are worlds apart and excluding people like Sly And The Family Stone or Kool And The Gang, they rarely cross over.

Soul is music of the heart and rock is music of the head, it's as simple as that. Rock is white music, soul is black music. At least it was that simple until recently with the advent of more and more blue-eyed soul singers.

Foremost amongst them must be Howard W. Casey, better known as K.C. of the Sunshine Band, who has individually pioneered a new course for soul music to go in with the emergence of the sunshine sound of Florida.

Apart from his own considerable hits he is also responsible for the gigantic success of George McCrae.

Then there's the sound of Philadelphia and such stars as the Three Degrees, O Jays, Intruders, and The Tymes. The list is seemingly endless.

Something else that has grown enormously in popularity in the last few years has been the sound of the West Indies. Reggae.

The insidious chugging beat and crossed rhythms make it one of the finest forms of music to dance to, and discotheques are breaking the records very quickly.

The upsurge in soul has given birth to many associated phenomena, not the least being the Northern soul clubs where young people got to dance all night long to some of the blackest and fastest music on the scene today.

The most famous, and most respected of these clubs is the Wigan Casino, where especially rare discs, some selling for a small fortune, are played by some of the most knowledgeable people in the business.

Yes, soul has come a long way since its Mississippi delta days, and now it has so much momentum it is bound to increase in popularity. It's black, it's defiant, it's beautiful.

BRYAN FERRY has been revered as the darling of the poseur set—the man who continues the swashbuckling suavity of Errol Flynn and Clark Gable.

He's tall, dark, handsome and charming, and the Times has called him "the first man to bring a real intelligence to bear on pop."

His considerable musical talents aside, Bryan Ferry, with his tastefully-knotted tie, was the pioneer who brought elegance back to rock.

When he formed Roxy Music he had a band which effectively broke out of rock's increasingly restrictive conventions. They developed an utterly new style by blending past and present rock idioms with an experimental technique.

Right from the start Bryan Ferry captured attention. An honours degree in Fine Art, composer of Roxy's songs and possessor of a recognisable singing style.

He is very much a rock star to love or hate. Some believe his image, like his music involves no contrivance; that he can appear one moment in dinner jacket and cummerbund, the next in T-shirt and sneakers.

Others think that the whole thing is camouflage—a sham. The showbusiness master who has everyone fooled and running in the wrong direction at the same time.

One thing they are agreed on is that few performers have projected so strong and original an image which is also so versatile and varied in detail.

It was with the release of his solo albums that Bryan became a force to be reckoned with on his own.

His re-working of classic pop songs caught everyone on the wrong foot and led to a spate of imitators—a sure sign of importance.

He sold out the Albert Hall for a solo concert wearing a quiet suit and white shirt—quite a contrast to the South American gaucho image he had previously thrust on the audience who went to see Roxy Music.

Critics couldn't come to terms with Ferry apparently heaping one outrage on top of another and finding that it was all working.

Once when asked about which direction his future solo releases would take, he replied: "I'm looking for more songs to destroy."

Always fastest to the quip, it's Ferry's self-assurance that has managed to keep him ahead of the rest of the pack, with songs that span the whole emotional field yet always emphasise the need for everyone to have a lot of fun out of life.

He is a devastatingly unique star who may not yet have reached the pinnacle of his success.

SUAVITY LIVES

courtesy of Bryan Ferry

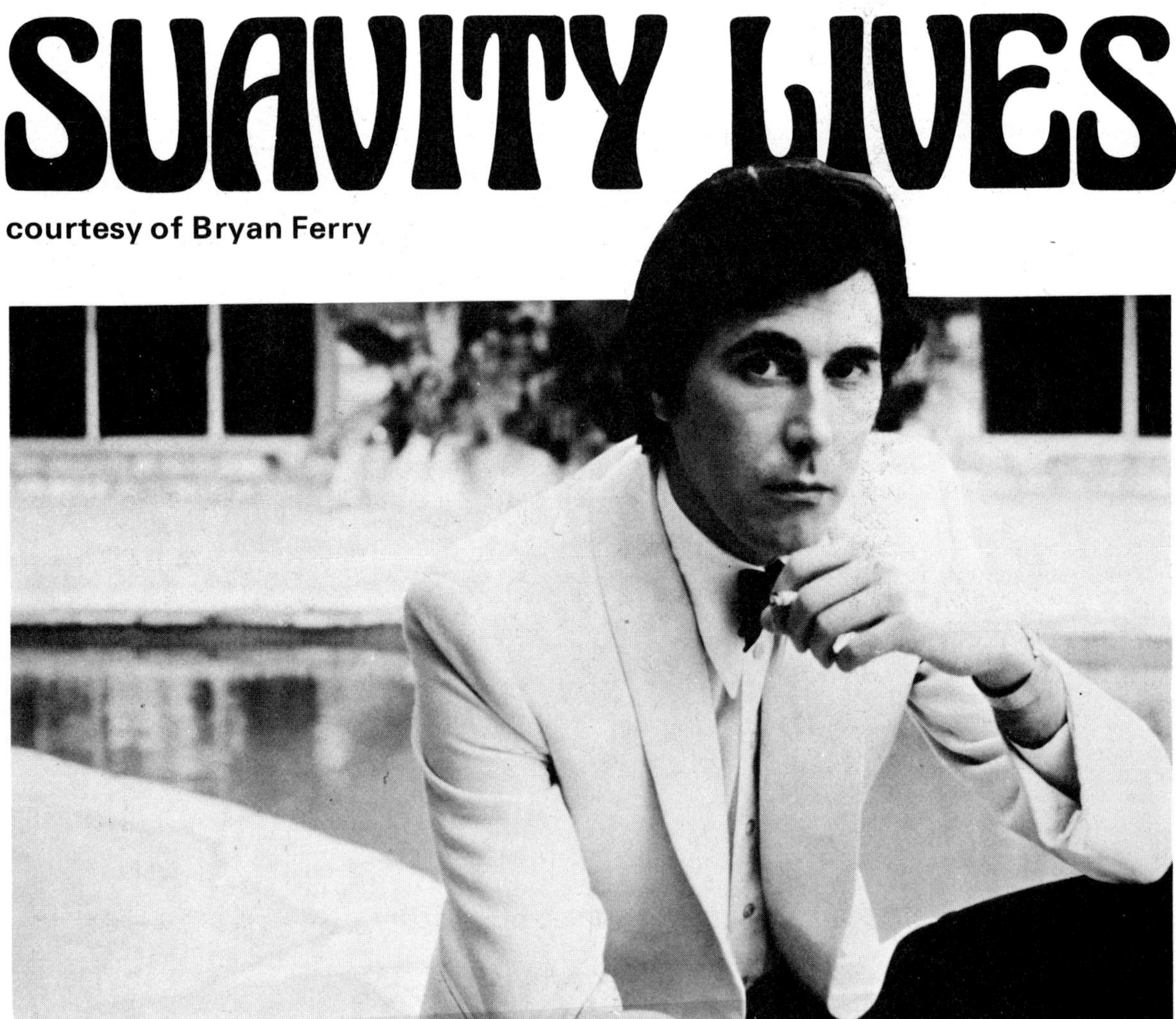

BRYAN FERRY

STEVE HARLEY

DAVID ESSEX

QUEEN

SPARKS

BAY CITY ROLLERS

ROD STEWART

JACKSON 5

THE JACKSON 6

AT A time when pop music looked as if it was falling into the doldrums, one man single-handedly put back all the old razzamatazz and flash. He is, of course, Gary Glitter.

By now everyone knows his early history of how he'd been in the business for 12 years as Paul Raven before making his big break in 1971 with Rock And Roll Parts One And Two.

But his real name is Paul Gadd and just for the record, he's 31 years old.

So how come all the glitter and flash?

"Well," says Gary. "When I was young, all the community used to hold fancy dress balls and I suppose some of it rubbed off on me because of the fantasy. Now when I do a concert I dress up and Glitter along and so do the fans.

"I look at the early pictures of me, when I was struggling around as Paul Raven, and the suits are sombre, the haircut ordinary and the general image was earnest, anxious to please, but boring. But I learned a lot in those days . . ."

He said in one interview: "When I went round the music publishers, I'd never be offered any of the potential hit songs. I was at the bottom of the ladder so I got the dregs. Now they'd probably bring out the brandies and the Lew Grade

cigars, but I couldn't care less . . .

"I started getting decent material to sing when I linked up with my manager Mike Leander."

And what a pop marriage that was to turn out to be.

Leander is one of the most astute managers and songwriters in the business, and between them Mike and Gary have built a pop empire of glitter with an instantly recognisable sound.

And to go with the Gary Glitter image, which won instant admiration from Liberace, there was a stage show of spectacular proportions not seen since the heyday of Hollywood. Gary was putting the show back into showbusiness.

But there was no hype. Gary is the first to admit that all along he's just a performer, someone playing the part of Gary Glitter.

He says of himself: "My style now is raw, crude, earthy, but it is all based on the rocking excitement I grew up with. I wear fancy clothes, but in the old days too the rock artists were flash personalities.

"I lead a fantasy life when I'm being Gary Glitter, but I share that fantasy gladly with anyone who will listen."

Yet for all his honesty it is only this year that he has come to be accepted by the majority of the music press.

Before, rock musicians and supposedly informed disc jockeys would sneer at his music as only fit for teeny-boppers. Now a great many of them are taking him much more seriously as he notches up hit after hit and moves towards that superstar status.

He's had to put up with a lot of nastiness about the songs he sings, especially with complaints about the banality of the songs.

Yet he's also received some back-handed compliments. Like the Sunday Times colour supplement for instance, which printed: "Gary Glitter can sell a million copies of a record whose entire lyric seems to consist of 'hey, hey, hey'. He is undoubtedly THE BEST 'hey, hey, hey' man in the business".

Gary is the first person to put down pretension. He says: "I don't go for telling people that there's something of real depth hidden away in my records—you know, tapping the side of the nose as much as to say it's there, real philosophic treasures, if only you were bright enough to find it.

"I'm saying that if my records help a party go with a swing, then that's good enough for me. I've said it's mindless music, but damn it all, pop music can surely appeal to other parts of the person than the mind."

Strong stuff from a star well aware of his talent and his limitations.

Now Gary has branched out into a different type of venture—a large scale musical touring show.

"I wanted to present something totally spectacular and the one-nighter didn't give me enough scope," he says.

He'll be moving more into movies because he savours the challenge of proving to people that he can act a bit, and looks set to become even a bigger star than he is at the moment.

One thing emerges when you look closely at Gary Glitter—for all the tinsel and glitter and larger-than-life shows, Gary still comes across as a real human being and not a manipulated cardboard figure.

He, more than anyone, is aware of his position in pop. He knows that he'll have to live with the "glitter" title all his life—no mean task.

Yet what does he say about it: "Oh, in the future it will probably come back as a nostalgia fashion like so many things and people will say 'remember those days when we used to dress up in the glitter, well that bloke Gary is on down the road."

Barry White the bear facts

BARRY WHITE is the giant of soul music as anyone who saw his concerts this year will be able to testify.

Not only does his mammoth frame and brooding, almost menacing looks, dominate any stage he's on, but his stature in the soul world is also tending to overshadow all other competitors.

Yet if you'd mentioned his name only three years ago it's likely you would have been greeted with blank stares. But Barry was around a long time before he met up with Love Unlimited.

Who, for instance, knows that when he was 18 he helped compose one of the all-time classic soul singles—Bob and Earl's Harlem Shuffle?

Or that he spent two years as a road manager for another soul singer Jackie "The Duck" Lee. And for the final twist Barry's been producing Lee lately, who now goes under the name of Jay Dee.

Oh yes, The Bear, spent a long time paying his dues before he reached the pinnacle of success.

Born in Galveston, Texas, 30 years ago, White moved to Los Angeles as a child where in true classic soul tradition he sang in the church choir.

As a teenager he took to writing songs and joined a rhythm and blues group, the Upfronts.

After years of working in the business things started to happen in 1967 when he moved to writing and producing for the Bronco label.

He worked with Felice Taylor on I Feel Love Comin' On but reckons the best thing to happen to him was when he met Diana, Linda and Glodean, the delightful beauties who make up Love Unlimited.

The rest of the story has become pop history. The Bear re-shaped the soul scene, with incredible production jobs of soaring strings on top of solid funk helping him carve a place for himself.

Never Never Gonna Give Ya Up and You're The First, The Last, My Everything have gone on to become classics in the soul field . . . and there are many more to come.

SHE'S GOT THE MUSIC

AS YEARS go, the last couple have been on the good side for Kiki Dee—and the band. After a career that's been going on longer than most of the bands and singers around today, Kiki's finally been accorded the kind of critical acclaim that a lot of people in the music business reckon she's been due for years.

For a long time, she seemed to be a sort of poor man's Dusty Springfield—and spent some time on the same label as Dusty—getting songs that weren't considered suitable for her more famous colleague. Some more time spent as the first white female singer signed to Motown and then a comparitive spell in the proverbial wilderness. It was about the time that Elton John was setting up his own record company, Rocket Records, that he heard some of her tapes and liked them and offered her a contract with Rocket. Apart from becoming close friends, Elton also gave her the kind of advice and help that she'd needed for a long time.

Amoureuse was her big breakthrough single, and then she opened up the Elton John tour at the end of 1973—an opportunity that she used to prove that she could more than fulfill any hopes the public had of her. She also got together a group of musicians who now form what is known as the Kiki Dee Band, and in one of the members, Bias Boshell, she also has a great song writer. 1974 saw the biggest step forward as far as public recognition was concerned: two tours of the States, the latter with Elton again, which took her across the country and back again. In many ways, that was her biggest testing ground. Elton is an even bigger phenomenon in the States than he is here, and opening a show with Elton as the star act can put off the most experienced of bands. But by sheer presence and talent, Kiki and the band had them on their feet and shouting for more. By the end of that exhausting tour Kiki had one single in the charts, and an album that got onto quite a few Best of 1974 album lists, I Got The Music In Me.

Early this year, Kiki went on a British tour, and also spent a fair amount of time in the studios.

One of the most under-rated talents Kiki possesses is her songwriting ability. Water, from the album I Got The Music, is one of the most beautiful tracks, and one of her own compositions. For someone with as much confidence as she has on stage, she herself is comparatively shy of her writing talents, and it's left to others to point out their merits.

With what little spare time Kiki has outside her commitments to singing, she likes to spend at home, but there is precious little of that. She loves shopping, but apart from that, keeps her private life as much to herself as possible.

Despite all the belated acclaim, Kiki is much the same as she was when the limelight wasn't on her. Her only ambition, ever since she was a kid, has been to sing, and for her it was the one way to escape the comparative prison of her background. She doesn't go in for star-tripping, and if she found that she was once again out of chart favour it wouldn't stop her. By her own admission, she says that singing is the one thing she can do well, and it's the only thing she wants to do. It's just nice that for once in a business where so many people succeed without really trying, due recognition has been given to someone who deserves it.

She's got the music!

DAVID ESSEX ...DOING IT HIS WAY

IN RECENT YEARS, there have been few rock artists who've been able to attract the kind of hysteria that existed in the days of The Beatles. The Osmonds managed it, so did David Cassidy, but the only British superstar to gain such adulation has been David Essex.

It all happened in the autumn of last year when David made his first full-scale tour of Britain. The national papers were full of stories of him being smuggled out of concert halls disguised as a policeman, of huge extra squads of police being called out in every town he played, of fans waiting for hours out in the cold just to catch a glimpse of him.

The mass adulation all happened very suddenly, but it had been brewing for a long time. David had already proved himself an all-

round entertainer with hit singles like *Rock On*, his role in the smash hit stage musical "Godspell" and his portrayal of Jim MacLaine in the box-office record-breaking films "That'll Be The Day" and "Stardust".

Success came after a tough childhood and adolescence. He was born David Cook in July 1947, the son of a dock worker and his wife, who lived in Plaistow, in London's East End.

When he was quite young, his father became ill and was unable to work, so David and his mother had to be looked after by the council. At the age of 12 he was to be found on Saturdays working in an East End open market selling fruit. He was a curious sight in those days, dressed in a cap, snazzy waistcoat and cravat and coughing his way through packs of Weights cigarettes.

Still aged 12, he was wandering round Soho one evening when he heard the sound of rock music emanating from a club. Fascinated he went it, stayed all night and came home determined to become a drummer.

After much cajoling, he persuaded his father to buy him a 30 bob snare drum he'd found and began practising in earnest. A year after he got his first job as a musician—in a band that played waltzes, foxtrots and so on. It wasn't ideal perhaps, but it *was* a band and he was its drummer.

After a few months he found an outfit more to his tastes—one which played Shadows numbers and the like. The group had a lead singer, but David didn't reckon him as much, so from his drummer's chair he began shouting out his own vocals.

The band lasted three years, during which time it played in France and Italy as well as Britain. Eventually, when the band was on its last legs, back in the East End again David was spotted by journalist Derek Bowman, who suggested he might be able to make a successful solo career.

David, with some misgivings, since he'd never dreamt of being more than just a drummer, agreed and for the next three years, under the new name of David Essex, turned out a series of ballad style records that did little to push his career any further.

He then began touring the country with an outfit called David Essex and Mood Indigo, that was so large it never made any money. In the end David became ill with bronchitis and was persuaded by his now-manager, Derek Bowman, to give up and try to get into repertory theatre.

He began to get work and slowly and painfully made a name for himself until, in 1969, he found himself understudying Tommy Steele in the London Palladium pantomime. The next two years brought him a couple of minor film parts and then in 1971 he auditioned for the role of Jesus in "Godspell" and got it.

In 1973 he was given leave of absence from "Godspell" to make "That'll be The Day". Suddenly David was back where he'd always wanted to be, in rock music, and had one of his own songs *Rock On* featured in the film. The record companies, who had taken little notice of his work in "Godspell" suddenly began to sit up and take notice—not because of the film itself, but because of David's song.

Once David was signed up to a record company, he was all set to be launched as Britain's answer to David Cassidy—but he was having none of it. He'd had enough of being a pawn of the business first time around and wanted to do things his way this time. He was in a position to get his own way too.

He insisted on being allowed to write and record his own songs in his own time, at the same time strengthening his position immeasurably by making the film "Stardust".

The pressures on him to tour while the going was good rather than make another film were enormous, but he resisted them and waited until he felt the time was right. The 1974 autumn tour, long

overdue as it seemed to some, proved his policy correct.

At the time he said: "You can stay away from touring for so long, but then there comes a time when you have to recognise that whether you prove to be good, bad, or indifferent you have to do it. That time has come."

Since then David has been careful to keep a tidy work schedule, not striking everywhere when the iron is hot and thereby risking overexposure, but sensibly spacing out his tours, record releases and finding time to pursue his film career as he wishes. After such a long and varied apprenticeship in showbusiness, it's scarcely surprising that he's learnt most of the lessons there are to be learnt and can see all the possible pitfalls.

The Sky's The Limit

GO BACK a few years in pop history, and it seemed that every other group in the charts hailed from somewhere around the Mersey Tunnel. Then as the pop world expanded a bit, there didn't seem to be any one place in particular that was responsible for producing top chart acts. The last couple of years have turned things around yet again, and this time a lot of eyes drift even further north than the Mersey and carry on up to Scotland—home of Alex Harvey, Nazareth, Bay City Rollers and the latest band—also possibly due to become the biggest of the lot—Pilot.

Actually, the links between Pilot and the Bay City Rollers are more than just patriotic; two members of Pilot used to play with them before setting up on their own.

It was back in '74 that Pilot, then just David Paton, Bi!' Lyall and Stuart Tosh, released Magic, which David had actually written three years previously. When interest in the single started growing, they made immediate plans to tour the country—and also added a new member to the band, Ian Bairnson, who'd helped them out on sessions for their album, called, appropriately enough, From The Album Of The Same Name.

Unfortunately though when the record took off, the tour was all set, and then after just one gig, Pilot had to abandon the rest of the tour because David fell sick with chronic laryngitis. At the time, the boys were all terribly disappointed, especially as they were due to play in their home town of Edinburgh over Christmas. After that, all their plans got thrown out, including a trip to the States to promote their album.

David finally recovered, and by way of celebration saw their follow-up single, January, hit the number one spot—in February! In a strange way, though, Pilot were a bit worried by the success—they said at the time that they would have preferred to have each successive single after Magic to go just that little bit higher in the charts. The pressures of getting to number one with their second single made them all feel that they were now honour bound to keep hitting that same place with every new record.

Strange things happed to them the day they heard they'd made the top of the charts—Bill Lyall, resident comic of Pilot, got stopped in a tube station and searched as a possible bomber because he was carrying a large suitcase. It turned out, much to the police's embarass-

ment, to be full of shoes and flowers from Harrods. Stuart Tosh was evicted from his flat the same day, which wasn't exactly something to celebrate, and poor old Ian was suffering from a stomach upset and couldn't celebrate even if he'd wanted to! And just to round the whole series of incidents nicely, David came out in blotches—all the fault of the London water system, according to Dave, which isn't nearly as clean and pure as Scottish water, or so he claims.

The sudden and enormous rise to fame caused the boys quite a few problems at first—especially with the constant requests from journalists for interviews, photographers asking for photo sessions, and fans who are just glad to see them.

"When we first made it, we were just permanently exhausted," David said with a rueful grin. "When I went down with a bad throat and we had to blow out some of our gigs, we were really upset, because we always try to fulfill and dates we've arranged to do. But people stood by us, especially our fans. The most amazing reaction from fans comes when we come home to Edinburgh—when they see us they tend to put one of your records on their record player and throw open windows and doors so that the whole street hears it. Also they walk behind us singing phrases of our songs and giggling. It gets a bit embarassing at times, but then if it wasn't for the fans . . ."

There are a lot of groups who have fan clubs, some better than others, but Pilot are very genuine in their concern for their fans. They launched their fan club last February through Record Mirror, and the response was incredible — with boxes of letters arriving every day. Pilot work very closely with the fan club, letting fans know of their plans and what they're doing, and using the club for special offers.

At a time when it's still fairly common for a band to emerge, have a hit single, and then disappear into the twilight zone never to be heard from or seen again, Pilot have stayed the course. There are often conversations between the people who are directly concerned with records and the people who make them, and Pilot were one of the few bands to be given immediate recognition. Not only are they able to make one hit record after another, but they also have the talent to write them themselves. It adds up to a lot of talent, and to a band who, having taken off, are still riding very high.

COCKNEY REBEL -Steve's way of making a point

COCKNEY REBEL'S origins can, in some ways, be compared with those of Roxy Music. Both bands were formed by their lead singers, neither of whom had been professional musicians beforehand. Both lead singers were the undisputed rulers of their respective bands right from the start.

Furthermore, both Bryan Ferry of Roxy and Steve Harley of Rebel succeeded in breaking their bands into the big league far faster than anyone had ever dreamed possible. There, though, the similarities end. Musically the two bands are quite different and it would be hard to find two singers with such contrasting personalities; the introspective Ferry with his style of studied nonchalance being almost a direct opposite of the extrovert, downright aggressive Harley.

Steve Harley began his working life as a journalist for a South London newspaper. He seldom talks about those days now, and though he found his newspaper experience interesting, considers it totally irrelevant to his musical career.

He describes himself as "a man with a heavy metal personality" and puts much of it down to the polio he contracted as a child, which has left him with a pronounced limp. Over the years he's developed a surface aura of being cocksure to combat his sensitivity but still doesn't suffer jokes at his expense any too gladly.

"Of course I have a chip on my shoulder about my leg, but if it hadn't been for that I wouldn't be the person I am. I have lots of chips on my shoulder and I think that if I ever discovered I no longer had any at all, I wouldn't be able to write songs any more." There seems little danger of that. He's only mellowed very slightly with success and his song output is in a very healthy state. He usually reckons to have about 50 songs lying around in varying stages of completion.

In the early days of the original Cockney Rebel, Steve was frequently accused of aping other artists. If that did appear to be the case, it was more by accident than by calculation. He very rarely listens to records by other rock artists and even more seldom goes to concerts.

"I scarcely ever set foot outside my front door except to drive to a gig or a recording studio," he says, "apart from the odd shopping expedition of course." Outside his group and his music, he lists his principal interests as girls and good food and admits to getting bored very easily. To prevent that happening too often, he keeps himself pretty busy.

Apart from fulfilling his musical obligations—writing, recording and touring—he's found time to write a book ("about my own life—I don't know enough about anything else") and make his acting debut in a German documentary film comparing the music of the '30s with that of the '70s. In it he's required to sing some of Marlene Dietrich's songs in a modern idiom, which suits him fine because Dietrich is one of his idols—"Show me a rock singer who could survive alongside her."

Most of the artists whom he admires first made their names years ago. He has little time for many of his contemporaries and often his own outspoken opinions on other bands have got him into trouble in the Press.

The first Cockney Rebel did not survive beyond two albums. Ac-

cording to Harley, the other members of the group had changed so that they could no longer work together happily. Perhaps the others would have put it differently, but anyway, in the early summer of last year the band split up.

Afterwards he said: "When the split happened I felt very lonely for a while. A situation like that is like the end of an old love affair, but you soon get over it.

Very quickly he got a new Cockney Rebel together and was ecstatic about it. "I'm working now with musicians whose playing thrills me and I'm very excited about it."

The new band played their debut at The Rainbow in the autumn of last year. "For once," says Harley, "there were no theatrics, no costumes, no hype at all. I'd toured with the old band not long before, so I really didn't need to do the gig at all. But I wanted to show people 'Here, I have a new band and this is how they play'—simple as that."

It wasn't until the spring of this year that the new band were seen on their first full scale tour of Britain and, of course, by that time the new line-up had made their first album together, though it was the third to go out under the name of Cockney Rebel.

Though Steve isn't one for modesty—false or otherwise—about his abilities as a writer and stage performer, he still doesn't claim to be any great shakes as a musician.

"These days I write songs more at the piano than using guitar, which I worked with mostly at the start. I don't play piano or guitar that well, but the piano and I are quite good mates whereas the guitar tends to make me angry."

"I'm not one of those gentle, subtle guitar players. I'm one of the sort that breaks strings."

Steve uses his anger as a controlled force. Before concerts he says he tends to work himself into a bad mood to get the adrenalin going and most people notice and stay well clear of him. Similarly, for interviews, he knows only too well that a cosy hour's chat doesn't necessarily make for good reading so frequently he allows himself to get steamed about and exaggerate wildly.

"I know I tend to overstate things and if people believed half of everything that I said, they'd get a very false impression of me. When I write songs, there's always plenty of time to cut out anything that's unnecessary and end up with what I feel to be important. In conversation, there's not the time and you often have to exaggerate to get your point across at all."

As far as his music is concerned at least, Steve Harley seems to have got the point over extraordinarily adroitly.

MOTT
-diary of a rock 'n' roll band

MOTT THE HOOPLE have had one of the most tempestuous careers of any band and, while the original group was an important force in its own right, in retrospect the band has come to be looked on as one that spawned an impressive array of significant new bands.

In the early days Mott, consisting at that time of Ian Hunter, Mick Ralphs, Verdon Allen, Overend Watts and Buffin, built up a good following but, in 1972 around Easter, they found that they were making no further headway and decided to split. That would have been the end of the group had not David Bowie persuaded them to go into a recording studio one more time and do a song he had written specially for them.

The song was *All The Young Dudes* and it gave the group the hit they'd always wanted. Bowie, helped by Mick Ronson, went on to produce the group's "Dudes" album and Mott signed up with Bowie's management company Mainman. Soon after that Verdon left and the band continued as a four-piece. Then, though, there was a lull.

David was too busy with his own career to pay much attention to Mott and eventually Mott felt their career couldn't wait any longer, split from Mainman, and produced their own album "Mott". This established that the group could write their own hits and produce their own records, but the pressures involved in doing so for the first time were enormous and, after it was all over, Mick Ralphs announced that he wanted to quit.

He departed on amicable terms all round and went on to join the new band Bad Company, which has since proved one of the most important new supergroups of the '70s.

Mick's place was taken by Ariel Bender, formerly known as Luther Grosvenor, who brought new life to the band, adding strength to the overall sound and bringing a formidable new stage presence to their live show.

At the end of 1973 a hugely successful British tour established Mott as one of the country's best bands and in the middle of last year they brought out their album "The Hoople", which added to their stature as producers of their own work.

Later in the year though, things began to go wrong. After a tour of America that won the band much acclaim and chart success, they began to have personality conflicts within the band and Ariel Bender decided to leave to form his own outfit. So yet another group was born out of Mott.

At this point, however, it looked as if the group would split again.

Then Mick Ronson came into the picture again. He had left Bowie when the Spiders disbanded in 1973 and had been pursuing a solo career since. It transpired that, while perfectly happy with the way his solo career was shaping, Ronson wanted the feel of working within a band again.

The arrangement seemed ideal and British fans looked forward to seeing the new band on a British tour just before Christmas 1974. Sadly, it was never to happen. Ian Hunter, who had not been very well for several months, suddenly collapsed with nervous exhaustion while on a lightening visit to America and decided, while recuperating, that he had had enough of the strains of keeping his band together.

Thus Hunter, Ronson and the remainder of Mott went their separate ways—Buffin, Overend and Morgan Fisher (who'd joined Mott as organist about a year previously) to find new musicians to complete their line-up, Ronson to continue with his solo career, and Ian Hunter to make a solo album and form a new band.

Thus, in the end, more new units were formed out of the ashes of a band that had, towards the end, seen great days.

They left a legacy of many fine albums to record their progress for posterity, culminating in perhaps the most accurate picture of the band's work—a live album, made partly in London and partly in America and mixed by Buffin with loving care during the last summer of Mott's existence with Hunter as its lead singer.

Hunter himself also left one of the best insights into the day to day workings of a group on tour—his book "Diary Of A Rock And Roll Star", which gives a good idea of the pressures that can build up towards a split.

IT'S IMPOSSIBLE to say whether David Bowie is a butterfly person who can't settle to anything for very long or if, on the other hand, he's simply a master of surprise. Either way it's always anybody's guess what he's going to do next.

One minute he's all for breath-taking theatrical rock extravaganzas, the next he's ditched them for the simplest of soul set-ups with no frills or props at all. He enthuses for months about the live album and film to go with it that he has in the can, then suddenly he's ditched the whole idea, recorded another live concert elsewhere and the result's out in a matter of weeks.

Then again, he'll disappear into a studio for six months, record enough material for four great albums, then scrap 75 per cent of it and emerge with one lone LP.

If all the changes of mind, the red herrings and the projects shelved are to make any sense overall, it is to be found way, way back in

1961. In that year a strange and quirky offbeat musical called "Stop The World—I Want To Get Off" opened in London's West End. It starred a young actor/singer/writer/director called Anthony Newley, who'd co-written the show with his partner Leslie Bricusse.

Newley had had a curious career beforehand. He'd begun life as a child star, gone on to play lead or second lead roles in endless movies of varying merit and then emerged quite by accident as a pop star by way of a film called "Idle On Parade", in which, for the first time, he was called upon to sing.

With "Stop The World", Newley suddenly blossomed as, perhaps, the first genuine all-round entertainer the '60s produced. So what has all this to do with Bowie?

Well, David loved the show and idolised Newley and determined to become an all round showbiz genius in much the same manner. The fact that Newley's precocious talent petered out rather sadly into a series of insipid film and stage shows didn't disuade Bowie from pursuing the vision that his erstwhile hero had presented in his heyday. Since then Bowie has always determined to have his finger in as many pies as possible.

Since "Ziggy Stardust", which set him on the road to international fame and wealth, he has been able to do pretty much what he's wanted and, though countless ideas have come to nothing, he hasn't been idle for a moment.

He's gone through massive tour schedules that would leave most other people ending up in hospital. He's worked eighteen hours a day for months on end in studios putting down a stockpile of tracks that would last him five years. He's taken a hand in record production for other people to help their careers on their way. Without him and Mick Ronson, would Lou Reed ever have had a hit album? Without him would Lulu ever have come back with the hit that *The Man Who Sold The World* gave her? Perhaps, one can't say, but the boost he gave to those two at least was enormous.

With his own career, the risks he takes are nigh on incredible. Remember when at the peak of his career in the summer of 1973, he had a number one album with "Aladdin Sane" and suddenly announced he had played his last concert *ever*?

Of course that proved to be not the case, but it was not until the spring of this year—nearly two years later—that he did perform live again in Britain. In many cases two years has proved long enough to be forgotten forever.

Last year, in America, he took a similar risk. He presented a highly acclaimed show on tour that was theatrical rock on an unprecedented scale. Then, having found a winner of a show, he calmly ditched it in favour of something completely opposite—a show where there were no changes of costumes, only the barest of props and where he ignored all but a few of his own songs in favour of a repertoire made up mostly of soul classics.

The reaction of the American Rock Press was one of horror. Critics complained that he wasn't a soul singer anyway and that it was not at all easy to distinguish one song from the next. Bowie was unrepentant and reputedly retorted: "I never give a performance that is anything less than great."

Since then he's made a resplendent return to Britain, worked with Marc Bolan on their joint film project and recorded a whole lot of material.

But what of that vast stock of material he's amassed in previous recording sessions? Ask him about it and he just smiles and shrugs his shoulders. Ask his friends and they'll say: "You heard some of them too? Shame, isn't it, that all those songs just lie there unused?"

Tony Visconti, the producer who has helped him so much with some of his work, says: "The thing about David that is so different from other people is that whereas they will break up a song into two or three parts to make three separate songs, he will mould four or even five songs together to make one glorious epic."

It seems that David can keep up his superhuman workload forever. As his wife Angie says: "David has a formidable energy drive. For most people it would be totally impossible to keep up with him."

Nevertheless, both Angie and David's close friends are often

anxious about his health, the problem being that he won't eat.

Angie: "I don't think he'd ever bother to eat anything if someone didn't put something appetising in front of him and make him taste some of it.

"The problem was quite acute two years ago when David was busy recording at Olympic Studios near London. Something special would be prepared for him each day at his Chelsea home and driven down to the studios for him. More often than not he'd only stop work for a couple of bites before leaving it."

Last year in America his secretary Corinne took it upon herself to buy bottles of every vitamin tablet he could need and forcing him to swallow the requisite number daily. If he does only live on pills-enough-to-make-him-rattle, coffee and French cigarettes though, he seems to thrive on it and long, indeed, may he do so.

A man of constant surprise

SUZI—A CLASS OF HER OWN

IN THE heyday of glitter Suzi came on like a black leather-clad panther, wild, savage and hard . . . or at least that's what everyone was led to believe.

Yet deep down Ms Q isn't like that at all and she's the first to admit it.

"There are those who say I'm very tough and all that, but I'm not you know I'm really rather soft, it's just that everyone's got this idea about me," she says.

Whether or not we've all got the wrong end of the stick as far as Suzi's concerned one thing is clear—over the past few years she's been the most phenomenally successful girl singer in Britain charting again and again and taking her hits right to the top.

And that, of course, brings its own kind of problems.

"These days I get recognised," she says. "Maybe I should be looking around for some sort of disguise!

"Take the other day when I wanted to go to the laundrette and I trundled along the street not at all looking like what people call a star. Then someone recognised me and before I knew what was happening there seemed to be an avalanche of people.

"What do you do? I just got scared and ran with my washing slipping and sliding all over the place!"

Just one small moment from the incident-packed life of the Detroit Demon who first started out playing in a band with sister Patti. That band was later to become a rock legend as Fanny—the first major all-girl rock band.

The world's most important female bassist says she didn't actually decide she was going to take up playing the bass.

"Patti formed this band, asked me if I wanted to join and when I said yes, she said O.K. you'll be playing bass. So then I had to go out and get one and learn to play it," Suzi adds with a smile.

Now she's on top Suzi knows more than anyone else that she has to work even harder to stay there.

"In personal terms the success means I can live somewhere decent and find some sort of private life," she will tell you.

"But I get so dog tired working harder and harder. I come back from gigs and I just flake out. When I'm not working I like to rest or amble round in comfortable clothes and do some reading. It's almost a luxury just to do that when you have masses of gigs one after another with little let-up."

For a girl who's already at the top Suzi still has plenty of ambition left and says she wants to go as high as she can in the business before fizzling out.

One thing's for certain, she won't be fizzling out just yet, and come to think of it there's not all that many rungs left for Suzi to climb, she's already in a class of her own.

DIANA ROSS

A SUPREME TALENT

IF YOU'VE ever seen Diana Ross perform on stage then you'll know all about her special kind of magic —her ability to hold the audience completely spellbound.

It doesn't matter if it's a nightclub or a concert hall when Diana's there she magnetises the whole place. That's top star quality.

In the days of New York's famous Cafe Society it was Billie Holiday who held that position but today the magic belongs to Diana.

As lead singer with the Supremes she was part of the most phenomenally popular singing group in musical history. Then she brought her versatile talents, sensual beauty and explosive energy to the attention of more millions when she played the part of Billie Holiday in Lady Sings The Blues.

When she's not bringing the Diana Ross Show to concerts and nightclubs, she's at home in Beverley Hills spending time with her daughters Rhonda Suzanne and Tracee Joy, her younger brother Chico and her great friends The Jackson 5.

One of the delights of her life has been the encouragement and help she's been able to give the Jackson brothers to find success in the tough world of showbusiness. Though Diana would be the first to admit that even without her help the talent of the Five would have eventually shone through.

The story of Diana is a story of a skinny kid from Detroit who said: "If I'm going to do something then it's going to be the right thing because I'm going to work with everything I've got to make it right."

And everything Diana has done has been so right that she's knocked over social barriers, leapt the generation gap and bridged musical tastes to become a top female singer in the world.

Diana is constantly working to learn more about producing and the business end of entertainment, constantly involving herself and developing her many talents.

Although only a tiny five feet two inches tall, she's an accomplished sportswoman, excelling at swimming and tennis. And according to Berry Gordy, President of Motown, she often beats him at chess.

You can put it all down to that Ross magic, which is another way of saying sheer talent.

THE OS

–A MUSICAL INSTITUTION

SOME GROUPS appear to go on forever, but, of course, none of them ever can—apart from, possibly, The Osmonds. If you thought little Jimmy was the last of the line and that one day, when he and the others grow old, there will be no more Osmonds, think again.

Already some of the brothers are married and it's not inconceivable that within the next dozen years or so there'll be a second generation of young bright-eyed Osmonds ready to take their place in the public eye.

Being an Osmond is being part of a family business, in which every member plays their part. Mr. and Mrs. George Osmond may not be seen very often, but they've taken it upon themselves to shepherd their offspring around the world and take an active interest in the business side of things.

The oldest Osmond brothers, now no longer able to take part in the group's work, still obviously pass on the experience they gained as members of the original Osmonds line-up to their younger brothers and sister.

The Osmond wives too, are not expected to remain in the background. They accompany their husbands around the world and cope with some of the behind-the-scenes work that there is for every group.

These days there never seems to be a chart around without an Osmond record figuring somewhere. Solo records, duets and group releases abound and, with so many different people to focus on, how can there be any danger of over-exposure?

British fans, it seems, can not get enough of the famous family. There are over 100,000 paid-up members of The Osmonds' British fan club, who all clamour for tickets whenever there's a chance that the group will be playing here.

Sometimes, despite the efforts of everyone to the contrary, things get a little out of hand. Remember the time when someone leaked the secret of when the family were due to fly into London's Heathrow Airport? There were frightening scenes with masonary collapsing and fans getting hurt.

That particular visit caused so much bad feeling and witch hunting to pinpoint where blame should rest that on their next visit, in the summer of last year, their arrival and departure were cloaked in strict secrecy and they chose, instead of doing live concerts, to do a week of shows on TV.

That decision won them a lot of respect for their sense of responsibility and also gained them many thousands of new fans among parents.

Since then, systems have been worked out to enable the group to tour here without all the troubles that marred past visits. Everything is run with scrupulous fairness.

The group's British fan club, run by an attractive young mother of three children, is one of the most efficiently organised anywhere. Everything is geared towards giving the fans value for money.

Ticket allocation is now worked out by computer to make certain that everyone is treated fairly. There are none of the usual falsehoods that sometimes happen in fan clubs. For example, if a competition prize is a T-shirt said to have been worn by Donny, then you can be sure that Donny has actually worn it.

The group are keen to personalise their relationship with their fans as much as possible and make sure that everyone gets a fair deal.

Mr. and Mrs. Osmond have made sure that none of their children have ever been spoiled. Everyone is expected to help with the running of the family's ranch home in Utah, doing everything from washing up to mending the stair carpet.

As is now well-known, the whole family are members of the Mormon religion and play an active part in the life of their church. They are also much concerned in charitable work for the deaf. The two eldest Osmond brothers, who featured in the original line-up, now suffer from deafness and that is why the family have chosen to become involved in that particular charity.

The group's appeal is very broad-based. While, when the group first found mass-adulation in Britain, it was Donny who attracted most of the attention with his boyish good looks, gradually the separate personalities of the other brothers began to emerge with the result that now some of the older Osmond fans have a special favourite among one of the elder brothers, while the very young fans are in love with Jimmy, with the girls anxious to hear hints on make-up and dress from Marie.

The image of The Osmonds as a close-knit family of good, wholesome people is a true one. The tasteless questions that sometimes crop up in press conferences genuinely embarrass them and are awkwardly hedged. They steer clear of controversial issues—anyone last year hoping to get a juicy quote from them on the Watergate scandal would come away disappointed. "We're musicians, not politicians," would be the standard and final answer.

No doubt if, in the late 1980s, there is a second-generation Osmonds group, the code will be exactly the same.

MONDS

MOST BANDS, if they exist successfully for long enough, eventually manage to gain at least grudging respect from all record buyers and the rock media as well. With the Sweet though, this has never quite happened.

As Sweet began to woo older fans with sophisticated singles like *The Six Teens*, they started to get complaints from their younger followers in the process and while most bands thrive on the publicity they receive, Sweet have survived almost despite theirs.

They ran into trouble at the very outset of their chart career. Critics, who loathed such candyfloss material as *Coco* and *Funny Funny*, were only too delighted to discover that the playing on Sweet's early hits was not all their own work and made capital out of it.

The publicity that piece of information received did the group untold damage and, long after it was generally acknowledged that Sweet singles were all Sweet, they still hadn't lived it down.

Although, despite adverse press coverage, they quickly built up a huge following with younger fans, they never got through to the mums and dads. As one of their songwriters, Mike Chapman, said: "Sweet were never the kind of boys a girl could easily take home to meet their parents. On TV they always looked just a little bit evil."

True. Parents forced into enduring "Top Of The Pops" by their children would undoubtedly greet bass guitarist Steve Priest's Minnie-Ha-Ha antics for *Wig Wam Bam* with snorts of derision. The Press too did not react kindly to such gimmicks and Sweet, after a run of number one hits, had only to go to number two to be told they were slipping.

Eventually, having proved that, with the aid of their songwriters Chinn and Chapman, they could go on producing hugely commercial singles for as long as they pleased, they decided to be more adventuresome and take a few risks in the process.

The first move was the single *The Six Teens*, which was undoubtedly their best ever up to that time. That one, however, didn't do quite as well as its predecessors and only added fuel to the talk that Sweet were on the way out.

Pretty much at the same time as *The Six Teens* came out last year, Sweet released their much-publicised "Sweet Fanny Adams" album. It was the first non-compilation album they'd ever made and, while it proved they were no mean musicians and sold well over a period of time, it didn't enjoy quite the chart success that had been anticipated. More talk of Sweet on the way out.

At this point the group's lead singer Brian Connolly took it upon himself to answer the question: "Are Sweet's days numbered?"

He said that he didn't care if Sweet never had a number one hit

single ever again. After all, they had done it in the past and what was the point in continually chasing something you couldn't better?

"Even if everything went wrong," he added, "we'd keep smiling. We're not penniless and we're very much into what we are doing—music-wise, writing-wise and production-wise, so I can't see a sudden end anywhere."

In November last year Sweet released their follow-up LP to "Sweet Fanny Adams". Titled "Desolation Boulevard", it scarcely set the world alight at the cash registers, but as far as the group were concerned, it pointed the way ahead.

"Our next goal," said Connolly at the time, "is to gain popularity as an album band. We've banged out singles for long enough. I'm not saying that we'll scrap doing singles—if a song comes along that's good enough to keep our singles-buying public happy we'll put it out, but singles will be of secondary importance to us.

"We're still feeling our way as far as albums are concerned, but hopefully, in four or five LPs time, we'll be ready to do a concept album and make it work."

To befit their new direction, Sweet toned down their costumes and deliberately set out to play to older audiences at colleges and universities, even if they couldn't fill these venues as certainly as they could those on a ballroom tour.

Gradually, after leaving the easy road, Sweet have begun to make their mark in a more sophisticated market, but they recognise that they can only progress as fast as people are prepared to forget what's gone before.

Fortunately, during the uncomfortable transition period in Britain they left one trump card to play. For years they had put off making their first visit to America, although they'd had enough hits there to more than justify going and there had been promoters crying out for them to make the trip.

Whenever asked why they didn't go to America, Connolly would answer: "Out there they've no preconceived notions about us. They know very little about us at all apart from the impression they've gained from the singles that have been hits there. Certainly they don't think of us as a teenybop band."

This year they finally decided that the time was right and at last went to The States. Of course, being such a huge country, it takes time to make an impression nationally, but already the signs are that it will happen.

Perhaps when they've finally won the respect out there that has for so long eluded them in this country, they'll be able to return via the back door with a clean slate at last. That's the aim, at any rate, and only time will tell if they can actually pull it off. In the meantime, as Brian Connolly says, they 'keep smiling'.

SWEET ...smiling through it all

PAPER LACE

MOST ACTS that become a hit on Opportunity Knocks and then have a subsequent smash record, generally fade away from the scene just as quickly as they came.

But there is an exception—Paper Lace.

They won the show twice and took part in the all-winners programme.

Lucky for them, Peter Callender was looking in and as a result the group were signed to Callender and Mitch Murray's record label. They were given a Callender/Murray song, Billy Don't Be A Hero, and the rest is history.

But their rise to stardom wasn't quite such a fairy tale as it first appears. For a start they applied to Opportunity Knocks about two years before they actually appeared on it.

Founder member and drummer Phil Wright recalls: "We auditioned in a Nottingham hotel and afterwards Hughie Green said we were O.K. Six months later we got a letter saying we'd passed the audition but nothing to say we were on the show.

"But then we got another saying we were on, and that was it."

Not half. Then they went on to take America by storm with their Night Chicago Died, to assure record buyers all over the world that Paper Lace had arrived.

Today their records sell all over the globe and they are constantly in demand for tours and gigs, but they are still the closely knit band they always were back in their early Nottingham days.

Once they even turned down £20,000 to be together.

Cliff Fish explains how his wife was expecting a baby—their first child—and the group were booked to tour Australia and New Zealand.

"I didn't really want to leave her and so I asked the other members of the band if they'd mind cancelling the tour. You know what, they didn't mind at all.

"So I suppose we've probably got the most expensive baby in pop history," he calmly adds.

So just how do they judge how good the songs they record are going to be.

"It's strange really," says Cliff. "We just hear a couple of lines and can tell if it's going to be good or not. Mitch and Pete say they've got an idea for a song, play a couple of lines of melody and you can tell the feel of the songs from those lines."

"Generally what we're trying to do is put a class image over with our songs and stage performance, says Phil. "We want to appeal to all markets, though I suppose some rock musicians think our music a bit of a joke."

Whether or not the Lace's music is a joke, one thing's for sure, a lot of musicians envy their success.

NEIL SEDAKA is in every way an odd man out in today's music scene. His recipe for success takes no account of what tastes are in fashion at any particular time and has no image ingredient at all.

"I don't care what writers chose to say about my looks at all," he says. "They can say I look like a bank manager or everybody's favourite uncle or that I'm tubby and getting on in years and I don't mind. Sooner or later they get around to the music and that's what's important."

The music, as much as his looks, has little to do with most of what is good. Sedaka's stock-in-trade is good old-fashioned melody allied to lyrics that encompass every well-tried subject from the unashamed tearjerker to stories about the joys of the seasons.

But, though on the surface everything about Neil's work may seem corny, he has the respect of virtually any critic you might care to name and his fans range in age from quite tiny tots to pensioners. Also, many a singer of international renown has had cause in the past to bless the day he or she recorded a Sedaka number.

The secret of his success lies in his unique talent to come up with an old-fashioned tune that's better than any other around at the time. As far as his words are concerned, he somehow always manages to make his tearjerkers poignant without being gross and to write love stories that are never ham.

As a concert performer, Neil is known for total professionalism allied to an irrepressibly vivacious personality. The latter has stood him in good stead during the lean period he suffered after a string of early hits.

As a writer of songs for other people he has never, in the whole of his long career, hit a bad patch but there was a time when people didn't want to know about Neil Sedaka as an artist in his own right.

After the first big flush of success that produced hits like *Oh Carol*, *Happy Birthday Sweet Sixteen*, *Breaking Up Is Hard To Do* and *Calendar Girl* he came to be looked on as an old-timer who'd had his day and ought to move over and make way for new, younger faces.

"At that time I used to get offered nothing but slots on revival tours," he recalls, "and I wouldn't do them at any price. Somehow I knew that sooner or later my new songs would get through."

Britain was the first country to recognise the 'new' Sedaka and it was here that he began to enjoy hits again both with his singles and albums like "The Tra-La Days Are Over" and "Laughter In The Rain".

Acceptance second time around in his own country, The States, did not come until much later—the late summer/early autumn of last year when "Laughter In The Rain" took off, months after it had been a hit this side of the Atlantic.

Perhaps it was the release of his brilliant "Overnight Sensation" album in the spring of this year that finally confirmed Neil Sedaka as a worldwide star. Since then, with new recordings and many more thousand miles of travel, he has simply been consolidating his position.

Neil Sedaka ...the tra-la days go on

Away from the concert platform Neil Sedaka is a very home-loving person. Whenever possible, his wife and young son and daughter accompany him on his travels. He hates living out of suitcases so whenever he comes to Britain for a fairly lengthy stay, he rents a flat in London for himself, his family and their cook. Often he's been known to travel hundreds of miles after a gig just to be home for the night.

A London visit by the Sedakas would not be complete without one of the famous parties they invariably throw for their friends, who after being wined and dined, can be sure of a free concert to round of the evening, with the tra-la day going far into the tra-la night.

WINGS

...you can't keep a good band down

WINGS' WORLD tour earlier this year must be looked on not just as a brilliant success for the band as a whole, but a personal triumph for Paul McCartney.

For him to form a major band in the wake of The Beatles and keep it going was a major achievement in itself. Not only did he have to cope with early teething troubles within the new band, involving several changes of line-up in its early days, but also endure many outside hassles. These included years of legal wrangling over the final dissolution of The Beatles, which almost brought him to the point of despair, and deeply hurtful criticism of his wife's role in his musical career.

Often Paul was powerless to help her in the first difficult days and had to leave her to answer for herself the allegations that she was interfering where she had no business and that, as a non-musician, she should have stayed clear of the band altogether.

It was perhaps only through seeing the silver linings in bleak situations that the couple managed to come through it at all.

For example, at one time there was some business trouble over the publishing of McCartney's songs and he sought to obviate it by pointing out that he was writing jointly with Linda. He was rewarded with the retort "She can't write". He then said that just because she hadn't written so far didn't mean she couldn't. This got him nowhere, the response was that she still couldn't write and what's more Paul could expect to be sued for £1 million in Britain and a million dollars in America.

Faced with this predicament there was nothing for it but to go home and persuade Linda to sit down and write a song on her own to prove she could do it. Linda obliged with *Seaside Woman* and has been enjoying composing ever since.

"For once," says Paul, "businessmen managed to do something good, even if they never meant to."

Although Paul readily admits that the years between the break-up of the Beatles as a working band and their final decease as a legal entity were "the worst in my life", the bitterness of the behind-the-scenes wrangles has always been kept much to himself. In interviews he has adroitly side-stepped any questions inviting him to snipe at his former colleagues and their various representatives.

When Wings were first formed, McCartney realised that to play their first concerts amid a tumult of advance publicity could do them nothing but harm. As a performing unit, they had no previous corporate stage experience and Linda had had none at all. He was therefore left with no choice but to get his new band 'played in' in hole-in-corner fashion playing unpublicised gigs to small audiences in out of the way places.

The problem of making a quiet debut in London was solved by springing a surprise concert on a totally unsuspecting audience at Piccadilly's trendy Hard Rock cafe.

McCartney never allowed himself to be ruffled by people saying that he'd come down in the world since his earlier glories. His usual answer to people who said that was: "It may not be The Beatles, but we're enjoying ourselves and it's early days yet."

The low profile policy paid off. Linda gradually came to be accepted as a worthy member of the group and her contribution to it has increased immeasurably, bearing tribute to her determination to earn her place in the eyes of everybody. Very soon highly respected critics were talking of Wings as the best live band to be seen in Britain and

McCartney himself was once again as much in demand for interviews as Mick Jagger. Usually one expects reporters to go to wherever the star dictates for interviews, but The McCartneys made a shrewd move and a lot of new allies in visiting the editorial offices of music papers to chat, not only to the interviewer, but anyone else who happened to be around.

Within the band, however, things were not always as they might be. There were various personality conflicts and differences over musical policy, resulting in inevitable changes in line-up. Despite these, however, somehow Wings managed to steer a straight course and with their album "Band On The Run" last year, finally came up with an LP that couldn't be faulted by anybody, and since then they've gone from strength to strength.

Clearly McCartney, who, with three children to care for, is very much a family man has decided that to work in anything less than a happy family atmosphere won't do.

"In the past," he says, "when personality conflicts have come to the crunch with a good old argument and people have said 'let's patch it up', I've said 'let's not bother'." It may seem a hard-hearted approach, but one can readily appreciate that, in the past, Paul has had more than enough of the bitterness that stems from unsuccessful compromises.

There is one legacy from The Beatles days that Paul McCartney is still trying to shake off and that is the persistence of some people in trying to find hidden meanings in his songs. That might seem a harmless occupation until you remember that Charles Manson, whose followers were responsible for the grotesque Sharon Tate murder among others, claimed that his horrifying philosophy was culled from the lyrics of Beatles songs.

Obviously that must have shaken McCartney, as indeed all the other ex-Beatles, and perhaps that is why he has chosen to release such patently simple, innocuous songs as *Mary Had A Little Lamb* and *Junior's Farm* just to show that his music is there to be enjoyed without any deep meanings, sinister or otherwise.

"As far as reading meanings into the words is concerned," he states plainly, "people really shouldn't bother—there aren't any."

Now that Wings has finally settled down after the early upheavals, which virtually left them starting from scratch twice over, one can expect to see some of the weight being taken off Paul's shoulders as the band's main writer.

With their huge world tour behind them and equipped with the prolonged experience of playing together that it has afforded them, they have had time to work in the studios again. There is now every reason to believe that their present and future work will prove their greatest test.

HIGHER AND HIGHER

THE RUBETTES were expected by almost everyone to be a one-hit wonder. Wonder they certainly were, but one hit—never.

In fact, despite personnel changes, the group has gone on to notch up a fair number of hits, each with that distinctive sound.

"It happened so quickly," relates Bill Hurd. "I've got to be honest with you, the Rubettes were just a stand in.

"Top Of The Pops had originally been planned for Sparks to appear, but unfortunately they couldn't get hold of visas to let them into the country.

"So really it was a very lucky break for us, and although it meant we were sort of second best, it also proved to be in our favour."

Of course, their distinctive white suits and caps helped give them an image.

"Oh those," says lead singer Alan. "Actually we were sponsored by a washing powder firm who told us that if we wore whiter than white suits on Top Of The Pops they would pay us a few thousand pounds.

"Nah, seriously though we designed them ourselves in the hopes it'd make us look pure and innocent like."

So are they more content now they've proved themselves as a hit band?

"Well, of course, we were a bit worried after Sugar Baby Love was such a huge hit. I mean, how do you follow that?" adds Alan.

"But by the time Juke Box Jive was a smash we were all a little more relieved."

For a band who were going to be written off as a one hit wonder, the Rubettes like their singing just get higher and higher.

THEY'RE SENSATIONAL

IF YOU'VE been lucky enough to see Sweet Sensation on stage, watched their professionally executed American-style dance routines and listened to their music, it might sometimes be hard to remember that the band hail from good old England—or Manchester to be precise.

It was back in 1974 that their name suddenly became a household word when their record Sad Sweet Dreamer shot to the coveted number one position in the charts. It had taken the eight-man band three years to make it, but from the time they first got together, they never considered giving up, despite the initial failure to get a record contract and more important, a hit single.

The youngest member of the band is singer Marcel King, now also firmly established as the fans' number one objective. Marcel started off by working in a delicatessen, but his ambition had always been to sing. A friend got him into a local pub talent competition and Marcel thought his big moment had come. He lost!

From there though, he was introduced to Leroy Smith of the band, auditioned for them, and got the job.

As a band, the first big break came when they appeared on New Faces—although one of the show's judges, producer Tony Hatch, had seen them a short while before, and agreed to work with them. Then they got another break by being booked as the opening act on the Mud tour of that time, and soon had Les, Dave, Ray and Rob singing the praises of their support band.

Snow Fire was actually their first record, written by the same guy who later wrote Sad Sweet Dreamer. That first record didn't take off, and as the writer, Des Parton, hadn't done much writing before, the band decided the best thing to do before he wrote their next single, was to travel up and down the country with the band, and see and hear exactly what they did. It must have worked, because they got to number one the next time.

Their follow-up, Purely By Coincidence, proved to one and all that Sweet Sensation weren't one hit wonders, and subsequent releases have only added to their fast-growing reputation.

Comparing the band with the Jackson 5 has been something they've grown to live with, although the comparison crops up less and less these days as they've established their own sound and their own way of doing things. In fact, with the apparent decline of the Jackson 5, the boys are now faced with the position of having taken over from their American counter-parts.

On stage, the boys never fail to get their audiences going. Their act is professional and slick, but when they're really getting it on, they tend to leave the practised dance steps for their more native Jamaican shuffle. And when Marcel gets into those falsetto notes, things really start moving.

The fact that their live act more than matches up to the sound they create on record, has meant a full work schedule for the band. For most bands this can mean disadvantages, and all the members of Sweet Sensation agree that the thing they miss most about being out on the road so much is that they don't have much time for their friends back in Manchester. However, they accept that is one of the penalties of success—and they add that it does have its advantages. They no longer have to hump their own equipment into and out of wherever they're playing—and another major advantage for Marcel is that someone does his laundry for him now!

Although it's a long time now since that appearance on New Faces, Sweet Sensation haven't changed that much. They still get a kick out of going on stage and performing, and they love being able to record in the studios. The days for comparing them with others are over—they've proved they're definitely a sensation on their own.

ROXY MUSIC —their dues paid up

SOME BANDS seem fated to be dogged throughout the whole of their lives by rumours that they are on the verge of splitting up. Roxy Music are one of them, despite Bryan Ferry's categorical statement: "As long as I am touring, there will always be a Roxy Music."

People don't appreciate that, while for some bands the loss of a player may spell disaster, for Roxy it only marks the end of one chapter in their history and the start of another. For a start, the band's bass players have always been birds of passage, staying only for a few months in some cases. Other players too may bring their contribution to the group's sound for a while, before moving on to pursue projects of their own.

This fluidity works because the band is not run democratically— and no-one has ever pretended that it is. Roxy Music is Bryan Ferry's band. He writes over three-quarters of its material and masterminds all aspects of its presentation from record sleeves to stage sets. No matter who may come and go in the band's line-up, Ferry is always there to make sure that the sense of continuity remains unbroken.

One might, equipped with a picture of Roxy as a benign dictatorship, begin to wonder why Ferry ever bothered to have a permanent group at all. In fact, at the outset, he was urged not to do so. When he first took the band's demo tapes to E.G. Management, they wanted to sign him alone to make an album with session musicians, but he wouldn't have any of it so they had to sign the whole band as it then stood.

It was a bold decision to put his foot down, because he ran the risk of not getting a contract at all as a result of it. One can only guess at his motives, but perhaps, not being a musician himself, he preferred to work with friends who knew him rather than undergo the harrowing experience of recording his first album with total strangers, who might patronise him for his own lack of musical pedigree.

Everything about Ferry would lead one to think that he'd been born into and brought up in an atmosphere of upper class privilege. But in fact he comes from humbler origins—a fairly typical Newcastle family. His post-school career began as a Fine Art student, before, by way of various jobs including one as a truck driver, he arrived on the threshold of a musical career by forming Roxy.

In those days he could scarcely call himself a qualified performing musician. He played piano in a passable dilettante way but that was about all. Still, there was time enough to improve on that. First of all there was something more important to be done. Everyone Ferry talked to in the music business told him it was impossible to get a band into the big league quickly from scratch. You had to pay your dues first, they told him, doing tiny gigs and building up gradually.

Ferry proved them all wrong, though he had to go dangerously into the red at the bank to do so. Be that as it was though, within only three months or so after the release of their first album, Roxy were playing the Rainbow and, not so many months after that, headlining there.

Once the initial burst of enthusiasm had greeted Roxy's sudden arrival, the brickbats began. People resented Ferry's success because he hadn't 'paid his dues', to which he responded that he'd paid them as well as anyone since everything he'd done from his art college days on had been geared towards the eventual realisation of his dream band.

Roxy survived all the critical hammerings, because it was undeniable that every successive album was an improvement on its predecessor. However, while the group as a whole got over the critical backlash quite comfortably, Ferry's first solo album "These Foolish Things" was unmercifully pilloried in the music press. Then, when his second solo album "Another Time Another Place" emerged, people grumbled that they'd preferred the first one. Ferry couldn't win and gradually he, both as spokesman for his band and on his own behalf as a solo artist, became less and less available for interviews.

Relations with the media thus deteriorated still further and Ferry became branded as impossibly arrogant and it was put around that he was such a martinet to work with that none of his players would put up with him for very much longer.

The trouble was that Ferry was, and still is, painfully shy and that shyness, which is betrayed in the uncomfortable nervous laugh which punctuates his conversation, has often been mistaken for stand-offishness.

For a long time he was repeatedly and genuinely hurt by some of the criticisms levelled at him, which he felt to be unfair.

Last year though, in the first trickle of interviews he'd granted in a long while, he began to say that he no longer felt quite so sensitive about the harsher indictments of his work though he'd not quite forgiven some papers for their delight in publishing ridiculous 'candid camera' shots of him on-

stage.

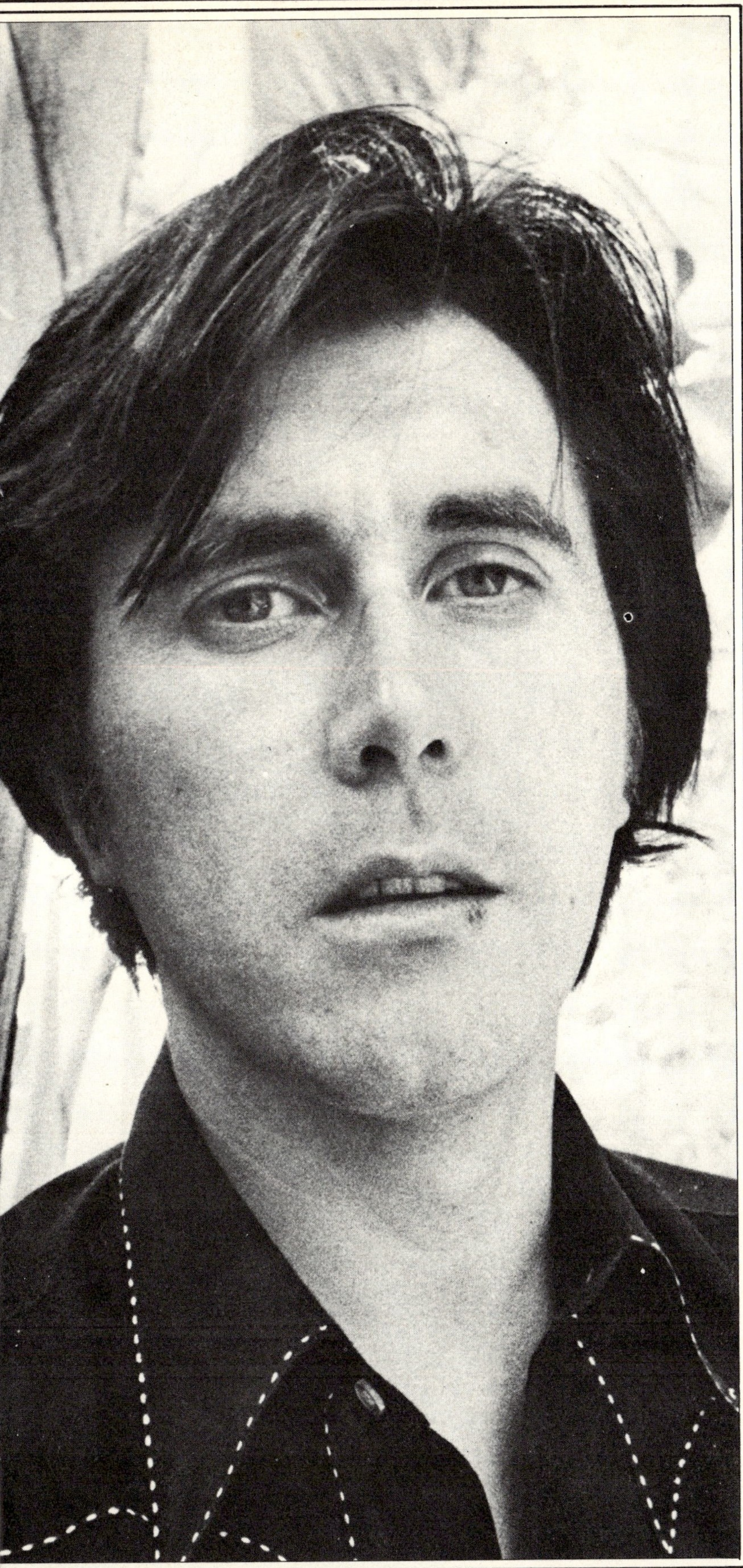

Despite Roxy's touchy relationship with the Press, they have never lost ground with their fans. The hard core that were there with them at the start has never dwindled and they have gradually won more fans with each successive new album and single.

In Europe as in Britain they gained swift acceptance—and kept it. Only in America, which usually takes the avant garde to its bosom very readily, did they, strangely, find they had a long haul towards finding mass appeal.

The first American visit, which Ferry and his cohorts had anticipated with such enthusiasm, brought only disillusion. On their return a dejected Bryan admitted that all had not gone as well as had been hoped. "They just didn't know who we were or what we were all about at all," he complained.

Later he decided that to make any impact the band needed to be reasonably well-known in advance. So it was that, before the second Roxy US tour last year, Ferry made an exhausting, whirlwind visit across the continent to pave the way with radio and TV interviews and by meeting as many people as he could. The policy paid off and the second tour made a lot more headway for the band than the first.

This year Roxy have toured extensively to consolidate their position in America and also set out to woo the Far East, with the result that now, after only three years of existence, they are as much a musical institution as any of Britain's longer standing bands of world-wide renown.

'76 CALENDAR

	JANUARY					FEBRUARY				
S		4	11	18	25	1	8	15	22	29
M		5	12	19	26	2	9	16	23	
Tu		6	13	20	27	3	10	17	24	
W		7	14	21	28	4	11	18	25	
Th	1	8	15	22	29	5	12	19	26	
F	2	9	16	23	30	6	13	20	27	
S	3	10	17	24	31	7	14	21	28	

	MAY					JUNE				
S	30	2	9	16	23		6	13	20	27
M	31	3	10	17	24		7	14	21	28
Tu		4	11	18	25	1	8	15	22	29
W		5	12	19	26	2	9	16	23	30
Th		6	13	20	27	3	10	17	24	
F		7	14	21	28	4	11	18	25	
S	1	8	15	22	29	5	12	19	26	

	SEPTEMBER					OCTOBER				
S		5	12	19	26	31	3	10	17	24
M		6	13	20	27		4	11	18	25
Tu		7	14	21	28		5	12	19	26
W	1	8	15	22	29		6	13	20	27
Th	2	9	16	23	30		7	14	21	28
F	3	10	17	24		1	8	15	22	29
S	4	11	18	25		2	9	16	23	30